Table of Contents

Executive Summary 1

I. Background 7
  A. Terrorism Risk Insurance Overview 7
  B. Report Mandate 14

II. Key Findings 15
  A. General Methodology 15
    A1. Economic Framework 15
    A2. Scope of Report 17

  B. Long-Term Overall Availability and Affordability of Terrorism Risk
  Insurance 17
    B.1. Measuring and Managing Risk Accumulations 18
    B.2. Modeling Terrorist Attacks 23
    B.3. Reinsurance 25
    B.4. Terrorism Risk Insurance Market 31
    B.5. State Regulation 49
    B.6. Buyer Behavior 55

  C. Group Life Coverage 63
    C.1. Group Life Market Conditions 64
    C.2. Reinsurance 67
    C.3. Measuring and Managing Risk Accumulations 69

  D. Chemical, Nuclear, Biological and Radiological Coverage 72
    D.1. Market Conditions 72
    D.2. Buyer Behavior 78

III. Overall Conclusion 79

Appendix 81

Terrorism Risk Insurance

Report of
The President's Working Group on Financial Markets

I. Background

A. Terrorism Risk Insurance Overview

Overview of Terrorism Risk Insurance Prior to September 11

Prior to the September 11 terrorist attacks, various insurance products that insurance companies sold to policyholders covered losses due to terrorism.

Insurance provided by property and casualty insurers is divided into personal lines (homeowners', renters', and automobile insurance) and commercial lines. Most commercial property insurance coverage is written through what is called an "all risk" or "all perils" insurance policy. Such "all risk" policies cover loss to the insured property from all causes except those that are expressly excluded.[1] There are a number of exclusions that have been adopted over the years, one common, long-standing one being the exclusion of losses from acts of war. General liability policies, covering third-party claims against the insured, generally work in the same way. Under life insurance policies, claims are paid upon death, with very few exclusions. An exception to the general exclusion framework is workers' compensation insurance, which covers work-related injury or death however caused, even if by an act of war or terrorism. Specialty insurance programs also developed to provide coverage for perils that were excluded from "all risk" policies. For example, aviation war-risk insurance, an endorsement to some general aviation policies, covers hull damage and liability claims from acts of war and terrorism, and specialty insurers have long provided coverage for acts of war, terrorism, and piracy in the maritime shipping industry.

While prior to September 11 most commercial property and casualty policies sold in the U.S. excluded losses from acts of war, generally speaking, most policies did not exclude losses from terrorism. Policies covered terrorism despite the fact that foreign-sponsored terrorist attacks had occurred or were attempted against U.S. properties prior to September 11, most notably the February 26, 1993 bombing of the World Trade Center ($510 million in insured losses[2]) and the December 1999 attempted bombing of the Los Angeles Airport by Ahmed Ressam (often referred to as the "millennium bomber").[3] Domestic terrorist attacks occurred as well, including the April 19, 1995 bombing of the

---

[1] A standard "all risk" policy usually provides: "This policy insures against all risks of physical loss or damage to property described herein, except as specifically hereinafter excluded."

[2] Swiss Re, sigma catastrophe database.

[3] Other attacks outside the continental U.S. but against U.S. territory included the August 7, 1998 bombing in and around the U.S. Embassies in Nairobi, Kenya, and Dar es Salaam, Tanzania; and the October 12, 2000 bombing of the U.S.S. Cole in Aden harbor, Yemen.

Alfred P. Murrah Federal Building in Oklahoma City ($125 million in insured losses[4]). From the perspective of insurance companies, September 11 was a realization of risks that had existed, even in the U.S. The magnitude, however, far exceeded general expectations. Insured losses from September 11 are currently estimated at $32.5 billion, including property, life, and liability claims.[5] Hence, the September 11 attacks led to an increased desire among insurance companies to exclude terrorism risk from "all risk" policies.

Industry Response after September 11

Following September 11, commercial property and casualty insurers began excluding terrorism from the coverage provided in new and renewing insurance policies, if allowed by state law. Aviation insurers exercised provisions in their policies that cancelled coverage. State law prohibited workers' compensation insurers from excluding terrorism. While not prohibited by state law, it is not at all clear to what extent life insurers excluded terrorism in new life policies. Reinsurance contracts excluded coverage for terrorism upon the next annual renewal, with the majority of exclusions taking effect in January 2002.

The actual timing of imposing terrorism exclusions depended to a large degree on the type of insurance company. For insurance companies subject to state regulation (often called the licensed or admitted market), new policy forms containing terrorism risk exclusions generally required approval.[6] For those policies requiring approval, a standard terrorism exclusion was separately filed by two major advisory and rating organizations – Insurance Services Office, Inc., (ISO) and the American Association of Insurance Services (AAIS) – and was approved by the National Association of Insurance Commissioners (NAIC) soon thereafter. In addition to these standard exclusions, some individual insurance companies drafted their own exclusions (some more restrictive than the standard exclusions), which were also approved by some states. The National Council on Compensation Insurance, Inc., (NCCI), an insurance advisory organization focused on workers' compensation insurance, did not propose terrorism exclusions as workers' compensation insurance coverage is dictated by state law.

The standard terrorism exclusion allowed losses from an act of terrorism to be excluded so long as the total insured losses exceeded $25 million. For liability policies, the $25 million threshold applied, but in addition, in order for losses to be excluded, the attack had to result in serious injury to fifty or more persons. Chemical, nuclear,

---

[4] Swiss Re, sigma catastrophe database. This figure represents insured losses and not total losses.

[5] L. James Valverde, Jr. & Robert P. Hartwig, "9/11 and Insurance: The Five Year Anniversary," Insurance Information Institute, September 2006 (also estimating the insured losses in current dollars at $35.6 billion). Property and business interruption losses alone are estimated at $20.7 billion in 2005 dollars. Swiss Re, *sigma,* No. 2/2006.

[6] Surplus lines insurers, whose insurance policy forms are not subject to state regulatory approval, began excluding terrorism immediately. In addition, some states exempt commercial property and casualty insurance policies from form approval if sold to large commercial policyholders (the public policy rationale being that these are sophisticated buyers); and in such instances terrorism exclusions were also put into effect.

biological, or radiological attacks, however, could be excluded no matter the loss level. Thus, small-scale terrorist attacks (below $25 million in total insured losses) were generally required to be covered.

By February 2002, terrorism exclusions were approved for use in commercial policies (that required regulatory approval) by 45 states, the District of Columbia, Puerto Rico, and Guam. Five states did not approve terrorism exclusions in commercial policies – California, Florida, Georgia, New York, and Texas – resulting in some terrorism coverage being available in those states. During this period, some insurers began to offer terrorism insurance, sold as standalone terrorism policies.

Terrorism Risk Insurance Act

The President signed the Terrorism Risk Insurance Act[7] (TRIA) into law on November 26, 2002. The purposes of TRIA were to address market disruptions from the terrorist attacks of September 11, 2001, ensure the continued widespread availability and affordability of commercial property and casualty insurance for terrorism risk, and to allow for a transition period for the private markets to stabilize and build capacity while preserving state insurance regulation and consumer protections.

TRIA established a temporary Federal program of shared public and private compensation for privately-insured commercial property and casualty losses resulting from acts of terrorism. The Department of the Treasury administers TRIA through the Terrorism Risk Insurance Program (TRIA Program). The TRIA Program was originally scheduled to expire on December 31, 2005, but as discussed below, the temporary program was extended for two additional years and with modifications. The overall structure of TRIA was retained, however.

How TRIA Works

TRIA essentially amounts to a government reinsurance program. Primary and excess commercial property and casualty insurers (including admitted, surplus lines, and captive insurers) who receive premiums for commercial property and casualty policies covering U.S. risks must participate in the TRIA Program.

TRIA Coverage and Limitations

The TRIA Program covers losses from certified acts of terrorism. In order to qualify as act of terrorism, an event must be certified by the Secretary of the Treasury with the concurrence of the Secretary of State and Attorney General of the United States. To fall within TRIA's definition and qualify for certification, a terrorist act must be found to be:

- a violent act, or an act dangerous to life, property or infrastructure;

---

[7] Pub. L. 107-297, 116 Stat. 2322.

- resulting in damage within the U.S., or to a U.S. air carrier or U.S. flagged vessel, or on the premises of a U.S. mission; and
- committed by an individual or individuals acting on behalf of any foreign person or foreign interest, as part of an effort to coerce the civilian population of the U.S. or to influence the policy or affect the conduct of the U.S. government.

Some limitations apply; an act can not be certified as an act of terrorism under TRIA if:

- the act is committed as part of a Congressionally-declared war (except that acts of war may be certified for the sole purpose of covering workers' compensation insurance losses); or
- the property and casualty insurance losses from the act do not exceed $5 million.

Types of Insurance Covered Under TRIA

TRIA coverage applies to *commercial* property and casualty insurance. It does not apply to personal insurance, such as homeowners', automobile, or life insurance. Commercial property and casualty insurance is defined to specifically include excess insurance, workers' compensation insurance, and during the first three years of the TRIA Program, surety insurance. (As discussed below, the TRIA Program was not extended for certain types of insurance previously included in the Program). By law, the TRIA Program does not apply to:

- Federal or private crop insurance;
- Private mortgage insurance, or title insurance;
- Financial guaranty insurance offered by a monoline financial guaranty insurance corporation;
- Insurance for medical malpractice;
- Health or life insurance, including group life insurance;
- Federal flood insurance; and
- Reinsurance or retrocessional reinsurance.[8]

Generally, TRIA requires that insurers make available coverage for acts of terrorism on the same terms and conditions as other types of coverage offered as part of their commercial property and casualty insurance policies. While TRIA requires insurers to make coverage generally available, TRIA does not contain provisions relating to the pricing of terrorism risk insurance coverage, but rather leaves pricing to whatever provisions may apply under state law and regulation, or to the free market for policies exempt from state rate regulation. TRIA does not require that a policyholder purchase terrorism risk insurance (although, as with workers' compensation insurance, state law may). Thus, if a purchaser declines the offer of terrorism coverage, the insurer can then exclude terrorism losses from coverage under the insurance policy or negotiate other limited forms of coverage, if allowed by state law.

---

[8] Other types of insurance were excluded from the TRIA Program beginning in 2006, as explained further below.

Although TRIA requires insurers to make terrorism coverage offers on the same terms and conditions as other coverages, insurers are not required to make coverage available for losses from a chemical, nuclear, biological, or radiological ("CNBR") terrorist act if coverage for CNBR exposure is excluded in the overall policy, regardless of the cause of the CNBR damage (*i.e.,* the same terms and conditions). Thus, insurers are not required to offer terrorism coverage from CNBR losses if such an exclusion is also applied to losses arising from events other than acts of terrorism, and if permitted by state law.

Insurer Retentions Under TRIA

If a certified terrorist act occurs, insurers may be eligible to receive the Federal government's share of the insured losses above a deductible, as specified under TRIA. Insurance companies will cover 100 percent of the insured losses below their deductible. The insurer's deductible, which has gradually increased through the life of the TRIA Program, is currently set at 17.5 percent of all the insurer's previous year's premiums earned from policies insuring U.S. risks (including the premiums of any of the insurer's affiliates in the case of insurance groups) through the types of insurance (referred to as "lines" or "lines of business") covered under the TRIA Program. This includes premiums received from all policies sold under commercial lines covered by TRIA, including policies in which terrorism risk insurance was not accepted. Thus, the insurer deductible is the same regardless of the individual insurer's terrorism risk insurance take-up rate. The TRIA deductible has increased from 7 percent in the first year of the TRIA Program to 17.5 percent in 2006, and is to rise to 20 percent in 2007 (though in 2006 and 2007 there are fewer types of insurance in the TRIA Program from which the deductible is calculated).

Insured losses above the insurer's deductible amount will then be shared between the insurance company and the Federal government, with the Federal share equal to 90 percent of the losses above the insurance company's deductible (and 85 percent in the final year of the TRIA Program). Neither the Federal government, nor private insurers will be liable, however, for any amount exceeding an annual cap of $100 billion in aggregate insured losses (each individual insurers must pay at least its TRIA deductible, however). Beyond that point, TRIA provides that Congress will determine the procedures and source of any further payments.

TRIA does not require participating insurers to pay premiums, rather it provides authority for Treasury to recoup its Federal payments *via* surcharges on the commercial policyholders of these insurers. A certain amount of recoupment is mandatory, based on insurance marketplace aggregate annual retention amounts specified in TRIA. In other circumstances, however, TRIA authorizes discretionary recoupment.

TRIA also contains tort reform provisions designed to manage litigation arising from or relating to a certified act of terrorism. In this way, TRIA addresses third-party liability exposure from contributions to personal injury or death arising out of, or related to an act of terrorism. TRIA also contains a prohibition on Federal payments for punitive damages under the TRIA Program.

Terrorism Risk Insurance Extension Act

The TRIA Program was originally set to expire on December 31, 2005. On December 22, 2005, the President signed into law the Terrorism Risk Insurance Extension Act of 2005[9] (TRIEA), which extended the Program through December 31, 2007.

For the two extension years, TRIEA modified the TRIA Program and reduced the Federal role in the terrorism risk insurance market in several ways. First, as noted above, it raised the insurer deductible from its 2005 level of 15 percent to 17.5 percent in 2006 and 20 percent in 2007. Second, it did not extend the TRIA Program for certain types of previously covered insurance, namely: commercial automobile insurance; burglary and theft insurance; surety insurance; professional liability insurance[10]; and farmowners' multiple peril insurance. Third, TRIEA reduced the Federal share of insured losses from 90 percent to 85 percent in 2007. Lastly, TRIA now has a "Program Trigger" provision that precludes any Federal payments unless insured losses from a certified terrorism event exceed $50 million in 2006 and $100 million in 2007.[11]

Two Commercial Terrorism Risk Insurance Markets

Following September 11 and the enactment of TRIA, two commercial terrorism insurance markets emerged – one for foreign acts of terrorism (committed by or on behalf of foreign interests); the other for domestic acts of terrorism (*e.g.*, the 1995 bombing of the Alfred P. Murrah Federal Building in Oklahoma City and the 1996 bombing of Centennial Olympic Park in Atlanta, Georgia). The two markets are also often described as "certified acts" coverage (based on the TRIA definition) and non-certified acts coverage (which includes domestic acts of terrorism and possibly foreign acts which are not certified under TRIA, depending on policy language). As terrorism risk insurance for domestic, or non-certified, acts of terrorism is not covered by TRIA and is reportedly available and purchased within both the insurance and reinsurance markets[12], this report focuses on foreign acts of terrorism. Although not the subject of this report, the functioning private market for domestic terrorism risk insurance (not including CNBR) indicates that terrorism risk is not inherently uninsurable.

---

[9] Pub. L. 109-144, 119 Stat. 2660.

[10] Directors' and officers' liability insurance, a type of professional liability insurance, remains in the TRIA Program, however.

[11] Prior to TRIEA, the only aggregate loss limitation was the $5 million aggregate loss threshold required to be met before an act could be certified as an "act of terrorism" under TRIA.

[12] Marsh, Inc., Research Report, "Marketwatch: Terrorism Insurance 2006"; Marsh, Inc., Research Report, "Marketwatch: Property Terrorism Insurance 2004"; U.S. Department of Treasury, Report to Congress, "Assessment: The Terrorism Risk Insurance Act of 2002," (June 30, 2005), pp. 78-79, 120.

Terrorism Risk Insurance Programs in Other Countries

Terrorism risk insurance programs with varying degrees of government support have existed or emerged in other countries. Even prior to September 11, some countries had established terrorism risk insurance programs in response to their own unique situations. For example, Israel developed two programs: one in 1961 to cover property damage caused by terrorism under which the government compensates for property losses resulting from a hostile act, and another in 1970 to cover bodily injuries suffered in terrorist attacks, as well as to provide compensation to family members of deceased victims. Israel's programs provide direct compensation provided by the government for terrorism losses as insurance companies do not retain any risk exposure.

In the United Kingdom, as a result of the attacks by the Irish Republican Army, Pool Re was created in 1993 to provide insurers reinsurance on amounts in excess of their compulsory retentions of terrorism coverage. Unlike TRIA, Pool Re is partially pre-funded by the insurance industry. Insurers pay premiums to Pool Re, which in turn pays premiums to the government when pool's surplus reaches more than £1 billion, and the government indemnifies up to 100 percent of claims above Pool Re funds. In Spain, as a result of losses from the Spanish civil war and long-standing issues with Basque separatists, an institution, *Consorcio de Compensacion de Seguros* (CCS), was created in 1941 to provide compensation for civil commotion losses. CCS was given legal status in 1954 as a government-controlled company covering all "extraordinary risks" including terrorism.[13] The coverage for these "extraordinary risks" is mandatory, and the CCS acts as the direct insurer by setting premium rates that are paid by policyholders as surcharges.

After September 11, other countries, most prominently France, Germany, Netherlands, and Australia, established permanent or temporary terrorism risk insurance programs that involve some degree of governmental participation. In several other countries including Austria, India, and Taiwan, private programs were established that do not involve government support.

A common characteristic of many government-supported terrorism risk insurance programs, including TRIA in the U.S., is a layered approach, where insurers retain exposure to terrorism risk below a minimum event size as part of a deductible and co-payment structure before government support becomes available. In some cases, such as Pool Re, the first level of assistance is through a pre-funded pooling mechanism, which is followed by direct government support. In other cases, such as TRIA, the government provides direct support once insurer retentions are satisfied, but then government outlays can be recouped through a post-event pooling mechanism. In the end, both structures utilize a pooling concept, but the timing of the assessments differs.

---

[13] These risks also include earthquake, tsunami, extraordinary flood, volcanic eruption, rebellion, insurrection, riot, civil commotion, as well as terrorism.

To date, other countries such as Japan, Canada, Mexico, Italy, Greece, Belgium, Portugal, Norway, Denmark, Sweden, Switzerland, Argentina, and Brazil have chosen not to establish government-backed terrorism risk insurance programs.

B. Report Mandate

Section 8 of TRIEA requires an analysis by the President's Working Group on Financial Markets[14] (PWG) regarding the long-term availability and affordability of terrorism insurance, including group life coverage and coverage for chemical, nuclear, biological, and radiological events. This section amended Section 108 of TRIA by adding subparagraph (e), which provides:

> (e) ANALYSIS OF MARKET CONDITIONS FOR TERRORISM RISK INSURANCE.
> (1) IN GENERAL. The President's Working Group on Financial Markets, in consultation with the National Association of Insurance Commissioners, representatives of the insurance industry, representatives of the securities industry, and representatives of policy holders, shall perform an analysis regarding the long-term availability and affordability of insurance for terrorism risk, including
> (A) group life coverage; and
> (B) coverage for chemical, nuclear, biological, and radiological events.
> (2) REPORT. Not later than September 30, 2006, the President's Working Group on Financial Markets shall submit a report to the Committee on Banking, Housing, and Urban Affairs of the Senate and the Committee on Financial Services of the House of Representatives on its findings pursuant to the analysis conducted under subsection (a).

How the PWG Conducted its Analysis

In conducting this analysis, the PWG was assisted by staff of the member agencies who reviewed academic and industry studies on terrorism risk insurance. The PWG was also required to consult with the NAIC, and others with an interest in terrorism risk insurance. As a means of meeting this consultation requirement in the most efficient and most transparent manner – and given the short time frame – Treasury, as chair of the PWG, published a Notice in the Federal Register seeking comments concerning the long-term availability of terrorism risk insurance. (A copy of the Federal Register Notice is included in the Appendix.)[15]

---

[14] The PWG (established by Executive Order 12631) is comprised of the Secretary of the Treasury, the Chairman of the Board of Governors of the Federal Reserve System, the Chairman of the Securities and Exchange Commission, and the Chairman of the Commodity Futures Trading Commission. Executive Order No. 12,631, 53 Fed. Reg. 9421 (March 18, 1988).

[15] Instructions on how interested persons may review the comments received by the PWG are found in the appended Federal Register Notice (also published at 71 Fed. Reg. 11460 (March 7, 2006)).

In addition to the comments received from the Federal Register notice, staff also met with insurance regulators, policyholder groups, insurers, reinsurers, modelers, and other governmental agencies to gather further information. PWG staff also attended a public hearing convened by the NAIC on terrorism insurance in which various segments of the insurance industry participated.

II. Key Findings

A. General Methodology

A.1. Economic Framework

As with other goods and services, the availability and affordability (or more generally the price, or premium) of insurance is determined by interaction between supply and demand.

On the supply side, insurers are in the business of assuming certain types of risks. In assuming various risks, insurers transform the risk of loss from individual policyholders across a wider group of policyholders that may be exposed to similar peril. The key source of revenue for insurers comes from premiums and investment returns. At the most basic level, an insurance company weighs revenue against costs to determine the insurance coverage it will supply.

A fundamental aspect of insurance is the selection, measurement and management of risk exposure. The risk selection process includes the methods by which insurers measure the potential for losses from individual risks, determine which policyholders and insureds to accept and insure, and to what extent and at what price they are willing to provide coverage. Insurers manage their portfolio of risk exposures in a number of ways: limiting potential exposures; allocating levels of capital (referred to as policyholder surplus for insurance companies); and perhaps most prominently through the use of reinsurance. Reinsurance is, simply put, insurance for insurance companies. One reason an insurance company purchases reinsurance is to protect itself from catastrophic losses that could threaten its solvency or, at a minimum, limit its ability to respond in a timely fashion to claims. The measurement and management of risk determines an insurance company's capacity to write coverage, defined as the maximum coverage it will offer at any point in time at a given premium, in all its lines of business.[16] The amount of capacity offered and the premium charged depends upon the risk of particular lines of coverage, with higher risk exposures requiring larger amounts of surplus committed and

---

[16] Capacity is determined by the target share of policyholder surplus the company puts at risk for that line (referred to as the surplus allocated to the line), the amount and cost of reinsurance protection, the risk of the line to the company, the policyholder premium, and the cost of raising or replenishing external capital. The risk to the company is the intrinsic risk of the line alone, including uncertainty in measuring the potential loss distribution, and the correlation, if any, of that risk with the company's other lines and with investment returns.

higher premiums. In summary, insurers' evaluation of risk, and their ability to manage catastrophe risk, are key factors in determining the supply of insurance in the market.

On the demand side, a business evaluates its risk exposure, manages its risk through efforts to mitigate losses, transfers the risk of the loss (*e.g.*, to insurers), and bears a portion of the risk of loss itself (*e.g.*, self-insurance). In making the determination to purchase insurance, a business will evaluate its perceived risk exposures and the uncertainty of this exposure – which may not be the same as an insurer's evaluation – any potential for post-event assistance from government, and the cost of insurance. A business then decides whether to purchase insurance, how much coverage to purchase and how much risk to retain, or whether to forgo insurance and manage risk exposure in another manner.

The insurance industry is also subject to various types of regulation by the States that can impact the operation of the insurance market. States regulate insurance companies for financial solvency in terms of how much risk can be undertaken. States have extensive consumer protection laws related to approving policy forms and terms. Some states also regulate rates for insurance coverage. In addition, private credit rating agencies offer opinions of an insurer's financial strength and ability to meet ongoing obligations to policyholders. Such ratings are important to investors and insurance purchasers as well as the insurers themselves. A strong financial rating gives an insurer better and less expensive access to capital markets, which has a direct impact on an insurer's cost of raising capital.

A common characteristic of the insurance market is that it generally follows an insurance industry cycle, characterized by periods of soft market conditions, in which premium rates are stable or falling and insurance is readily available, followed by periods of hard market conditions, in which rates rise, coverage may be more difficult to find, and insurers' profits increase. These cycles are often precipitated by loss "shocks," when claims are presented of a type or size unexpected by insurers. Exposure assessment and underwriting adjustments are typical insurance market behaviors following larger than expected loss events. Following a period of higher than anticipated losses, insurers and reinsurers typically react by re-evaluating their portfolios and risk exposures, often declining to renew or issue new policies until the company's exposure and appetite for risk is re-assessed. As prices rise, insurers and reinsurers rebuild surplus and new insurers and reinsurers enter to take advantage of the high prices; capacity is committed although it may be re-distributed in some manner as the result of their re-assessment of risk exposures.[17]

The same interactions of supply and demand in the general insurance market are also present in the market for terrorism risk insurance. Against this economic backdrop, this report evaluates factors that will impact the long-term availability of terrorism risk insurance, including coverage for group life insurance and chemical, nuclear, biological, and radiological events.

---

[17] David Cummins, "Should the Government Provide Insurance for Catastrophes?" Federal Reserve Bank of St. Louis *REVIEW*, (July/August 2006).

A.2. Scope of Study

Given the time constraints for this report and data limitations, the PWG conducted its analysis on the basis of *overall* market conditions, unless the report notes otherwise. Nevertheless, there are variations in market conditions that appear evident from available market data. Market conditions appear to vary geographically. While terrorism can be conceived as occurring anywhere (a message raised by policyholder groups during consultation); generally, risk modelers, and the market behavior of insurers, reinsurers, and buyers, suggest a perceived higher probability of loss, and obviously greater loss exposure in concentrated urban areas and around iconic locations. Market conditions also appear to vary by size of insured, as measured by total insured value and other metrics (a subject examined by the Treasury Department in its 2005 study and by others), and also by the type of terrorism (*i.e.*, foreign or domestic). Market conditions also appear to vary by risk to conventional and unconventional attack, which is discussed in this report. Conditions also vary by type (or "line") of insurance; and, the report examines differences between property and casualty coverage where appropriate; and group life insurance, which is specifically examined. Still, while from time-to-time throughout this report various market comparisons are made, the key findings are intended to address long-term, overall market availability and affordability of terrorism risk insurance with an understanding that conditions can vary across particular markets.

This report provides analysis of available data on market conditions for terrorism risk insurance – a marketplace which has included a Federal backstop through the TRIA Program since the end of 2002. As enacted by Congress, TRIA is a *temporary* program, and while it has been extended for two additional years beyond its original three-year term, it is set to expire on December 31, 2007. As the PWG's charge from Congress was to analyze *long-term* availability and affordability of terrorism risk insurance, including group life insurance and coverage for chemical, nuclear, biological, and radiological events, this report identifies the factors underlying recent trends in the market that can be expected to influence further market development in the absence of the TRIA Program, or any Federal program.

B. Long-Term Overall Availability and Affordability of Terrorism Risk Insurance

The key factors examined by the PWG regarding the long-term overall availability and affordability of terrorism risk insurance centered around the following: the ability of insurers to measure and manage terrorism risk exposure; the ability of insurers to underwrite terrorism risk exposure; and the consumer demand for terrorism risk coverage. Each of the key findings presented below relates in one way or another to these factors. The focus in this section is on terrorism risk insurance in general. While these key factors and findings in this report are also generally applicable to coverage for group life insurance and CNBR events, those topics are covered separately in sections C and D, respectively.

B.1. Measuring and Managing Risk Accumulations

The Importance of Managing Aggregate Exposures

As with any risk, insurance companies make business decisions as to the maximum amount of capital to put at risk for terrorism. Insurance companies estimate and assess their current exposures, compare them to current allocations of capacity, and then decide whether more or less terrorism risk insurance will be sold and renewed. This process leads to greater diversification of risk and less aggregation exposure for insurance companies. Insurers' decisions to supply capacity depend largely upon their assessment of the risk of loss. Catastrophe models – models of potential losses from large but low probability events – are used in assessing severity, the size of losses, and the probability of the loss occurring. To the degree the assessment is itself uncertain, insurers will respond by allocating greater amounts of given available capital to cover the added uncertainty, making the supply to consumers more limited and raising the price (to the extent allowed by law). Thus, absent the capability to assess exposure, as was the case with terrorism risk exposure prior to and immediately following September 11, insurers are inclined in the short-term to stop insuring the risk altogether (*e.g.*, no new policies, non-renewals, and the use of exclusions). Similarly, when an insurer's risk assessment reveals over-exposure, as occurred with general liability and medical malpractice insurers in the mid-1980s, it may pull back in certain markets. Exposure assessment and underwriting adjustments are typically observed insurance market behaviors following large catastrophes. Following a large catastrophe, or loss shock, insurers and reinsurers typically react by re-evaluating their portfolios and risk exposures, often declining to renew or issue new policies until the company's exposure and appetite for risk is re-assessed. Eventually, insurers and reinsurers re-commit capacity, although it may be re-distributed in some manner as the result of their re-assessment of risk exposures.[18] Thus, the ability to model and estimate insured losses influences availability of coverage over the long term.

Historical Development of Aggregate Exposure Management

Following Hurricanes Hugo in 1989 and Andrew and Iniki in 1992, the importance of using catastrophe models in managing aggregation exposures from natural catastrophes became clear to insurers.[19] However, despite relatively significant terrorist attacks on U.S. soil (the first World Trade Center bombing in 1993 and Oklahoma City in 1995), approaches for managing aggregate exposure and catastrophe modeling had not been widely adapted for assessing terrorism risk exposure before September 11. Prior to

---

[18] David Cummins, "Should the Government Provide Insurance for Catastrophes?" Federal Reserve Bank of St. Louis *REVIEW* (July/August 2006); U.S. Department of Treasury, Report to Congress, "Assessment: The Terrorism Risk Insurance Act of 2002," (June 30, 2005), p. 27.

[19] P/C Extreme Events Committee, American Academy of Actuaries, "Report to NAIC Terrorism Insurance Implementation Working Group on Ratemaking Issues Related to the Terrorism Risk Insurance Act," March 4, 2003; Risk Management Solutions, Inc., "Catastrophe, Injury, and Insurance," 2004, p. 3; PriceWaterhouseCoopers, Global Study, "Enterprise-Wide Risk Management for the Insurance Industry," 2004, p. 49.

September 11, insurers may have anticipated that their maximum exposure associated with a given property risk was much less than the full value of the property or that their casualty exposure was limited to a certain number of floors within a building.[20] September 11 demonstrated how a terrorist attack in a risk-concentrated area can generate catastrophic losses well beyond previous expectations and across many types (or lines) of insurance (referred to as a "clash" event). After September 11, it became extremely important for underwriters to identify the accumulation of risk going forward.[21]

According to the American Insurance Association (AIA) and others, since September 11, insurers have improved their ability to measure and manage their accumulation of terrorism risk exposure through use of catastrophe models.[22] As a result, insurers can manage their accumulations more closely than they did prior to September 11 and make better underwriting decisions.

Moody's reported that prior to September 11 insurers were managing their aggregate terrorism exposures solely by using pricing as an underwriting tool. Moody's observed:

> In order to manage their aggregate exposures, insurers have employed the lone underwriting tool currently at their disposal before renewals occur, which is to quote high prices for some risks in order to discourage take-up in cities considered vulnerable to terrorist attacks.[23]

At the time, risk models were in the early stages of development although some workers' compensation insurers had been monitoring concentrations of workers with regard to natural disaster exposure.[24] Some property insurers were also collecting address-level property data prior to September 11; however, it was the analysis of the data that subsequently changed once models were adopted.[25]

In its study, Treasury found that by 2005 insurers used sophisticated loss severity models to manage their aggregate exposure. As Treasury stated in its 2005 study:

> Insurers' ability to identify and quantify the severity of an event in terms of insurers' losses has improved greatly. In particular, insurers are much better able to assess their exposures or accumulations of risk for a given terrorist event on an overall and individual customer basis. This is important because it allows insurers to more effectively underwrite coverage.[26]

---

[20] Generally reported to the Treasury Department during the period leading up to the enactment of TRIA.

[21] American Insurance Group, Comments to the PWG dated April 21, 2006.

[22] American Insurance Association, Comments to the PWG dated April 21, 2006.

[23] Moody's Investors Service, Special Comment, "Moody's Surveys Insurers on Implementation of Terrorism Insurance Act," May 2003.

[24] Moody's Investors Service, *Ibid.*

[25] Liberty Mutual Group, Comments to the PWG dated April 21, 2006.

[26] U.S. Department of Treasury, Report to Congress, "Assessment: The Terrorism Risk Insurance Act of 2002," (June 30, 2005), p. 6.

One of the benefits of terrorism modeling is that it allows insurers to assess and manage their loss exposure, both at individual locations and for aggregation of exposure. By doing so, an insurance company is able to manage its maximum loss exposure by diversifying its risks so that its largest loss in any one location or area is lowered. Spreading loss exposure over more diversified locations and types of risk should result in improved management of maximum loss exposures, which in turn should allow increases in terrorism risk capacity for given amounts of surplus and could potentially lead to a reduction in prices.

Current Approaches to Aggregate Exposure Management

Today, models are being used by insurers and reinsurers to manage loss severity exposure from both foreign (certified acts under TRIA) and domestic terrorism, as well as conventional and CNBR terrorist attacks. Models can be used to assess terrorism risk at insured U.S. locations and globally. Models are available for estimating property, workers' compensation, and group life losses, although models have not yet been developed for liability insurance given the high degree of variability involved with potential liability exposure.[27] More specifically, in terms of managing exposures, insurers can use loss severity models to:

- identify multi-line concentrations within a radius or geographic region;
- quantify the greatest potential loss to the insurers' portfolio (from policies with terrorism coverage);
- assist in pricing decisions (advisory organizations also rely on modeling in determining loss cost loads);
- evaluate new applications for insurance against existing exposure in the same area;
- evaluate reinsurance coverage; and,
- assist in underwriting decisions.

Given the nature of terrorism, insurers generally seem concerned about severe catastrophic losses from a single large-scale terrorism attack or aggregated losses from multiple concurrent attacks and the risks these losses present to their companies. Insurers are collecting more detailed information about the individual risks in their portfolios, monitoring concentrations or aggregations within geographic areas, and managing risk across multiple lines of insurance.

When assessing concentrations of insured risk within geographic areas, insurers model loss severity exposure in different ways. With property exposure, most approaches calculate maximum loss as the sum of the full policy limits of all potentially-triggered property policies (multiple policyholders in the same building) and coverages (physical property, loss of use, business interruption, *etc.*), net of any policyholder retentions. Casualty line exposure, such as workers' compensation, is calculated based

---

[27] American Insurance Association, Comments to the PWG dated April 21, 2006.

on the number of individuals at the location and using statutory death benefit and disability award amounts. Deterministic modeling strives for a more precise estimate of likely losses rather than a maximum. Although methodologies differ,[28] some examples of modeling approaches include the following:

- Single-address or single-location exposure assessment – Quantifies maximum loss if a single insured property (*i.e.*, a single building) were destroyed.

- Landmark-based or target-based exposure assessment – Identifies exposure around a particular city block or near an iconic location. Modeling firms have extensive catalogs of these locations against which insurers can assess their proximity exposure. Over time, these databases continue to expand and become more useful.

- Aggregate exposure assessment – Quantifies maximum loss over very wide geographic areas. Although some insurers may not have the detailed or accurate policyholder data that is required for some models (such as not knowing how many of its policyholders are in the same building, or how many insured individuals are located in a building, *etc.*), most can identify policies by zip code, city, or county. Though somewhat less exact, insurers can assess maximum loss over these broad areas. These assessments do have some utility when evaluating CNBR exposure.

- Ring concentration accumulation assessment – Quantifies the maximum loss not just from the destruction of a single insured property but resulting from losses throughout a wider geographic area encompassing the locations of multiple insureds. After selecting a damage circle or ring that overlays mapped insured locations, maximum loss within the radius is calculated. Models can also identify areas of clustered insured locations in which maximum loss exceeds an input loss threshold reflecting the insurer's risk appetite.

- Deterministic loss modeling – Identifies an insurer's accumulation exposure from a particular attack footprint scenario. Deterministic modeling provides a more accurate assessment of the expected losses from specific types of hypothetical attacks in comparison to maximum loss exposure modeling. For example, a model could estimate the type and size of losses from a 5-ton blast occurring at a specific address. Deterministic models incorporate data about specific buildings in terms of

---

[28] For a discussion of various approaches, see Applied Insurance Research (AIR) Worldwide Corp., "Terrorism Risk Assessment: Best Practices for Insurers and Reinsurers," 2005; John Tedeschi, Krista Ann Lieman & Peter Cheesman, "Terrorism Modeling, Preparing the Worst-Case Scenario," Guy Carpenter, December 2004; American Academy of Actuaries' Terrorism Risk Insurance Subgroup, Comments to the PWG dated April 21, 2006.

building characteristics and engineering, surrounding urban environment (buildings around buildings), number of floors, occupancy, *etc.*

A.M. Best reported some specific statistics on the use of approaches to modeling loss severity in its 2004 terrorism Supplemental Rating Questionnaire (SRQ).[29] The SRQ asked companies what methods they used to measure their exposure to terrorism.[30] Accumulation management was used by 45 percent of respondents while 36 percent did not use the method, and 19 percent did not respond to the question. Thirty percent of insurers measured accumulation by proximity to landmarks. Deterministic modeling was used by 53 percent of insurers while 32 percent did not use this method, and 15 percent did not respond. Given the structure of this survey, it is difficult to make generalizations; however, it appears that at least 50 percent of insurers were using some method. In addition, as noted above, there likely have been further increases in the use of models to manage accumulation exposure since 2004.[31] Nonetheless, the A.M. Best SRQ does seem to indicate that there remains some room for improvement.

A number of commercially available modeling systems are available to implement the various modeling approaches described above, and some insurers have developed their own proprietary models.[32] The effectiveness of these assessment tools depends to a large degree on the collection of detailed and accurate input data. The American Academy of Actuaries' (AAA) comments to the PWG explained that insurers have improved their data collection since 2001.[33] In addition, Liberty Mutual commented that since September 11, it now requires workers' compensation insureds to provide specific employee information in order to geocode employee concentrations.[34] Consultations with stakeholders confirmed that overall there had been greater use of models and substantial improvement in managing aggregate loss exposure in recent years. Still, the AAA asserted that many insurers had room to improve their systems.[35] During consultations, representatives of group life insurance providers acknowledged (and studies suggest) that they lag behind in this area (see section C).

---

[29] A.M. Best, Special Report, "Terrorism: Too Risky Without TRIA?," December 2005.

[30] The study included responses from 155 rated primary insurers who wrote commercial terrorism coverage with TRIA-defined direct earned premiums making up at least 10 percent of their total written premiums.

[31] A limited survey of insurers by Wharton in the Spring of 2005 indicated a high percentage of model usage among large insurers. Wharton surveyed 40 member companies of two leading insurance trade associations; 12 responded, 7 of which were among the top 10 that represent 50 percent of the TRIA line market. The 10 insurers surveyed stated that they model scenarios in managing their exposure; 1 insurer did not; 1 did not respond. Wharton Risk Management and Decision Processes Center, "TRIA and Beyond," The Wharton School, University of Pennsylvania, August 2005.

[32] The leading commercial providers are Applied Insurance Research Worldwide (AIR), EQECAT, and Risk Management Services (RMS). In terms of proprietary models see: Lloyd's of London, Comments to the PWG dated April 21, 2006; "Insurers Can Model Terror Threats More Closely," *BestWire*, August 2, 2004.

[33] American Academy of Actuaries' Terrorism Risk Insurance Subgroup, Comments to the PWG dated April 21, 2006.

[34] Libery Mutual Group, Comments to the PWG dated April 21, 2006.

[35] American Academy of Actuaries' Terrorism Risk Insurance Subgroup, Comments to the PWG dated April 21, 2006.

Over time, as databases expand, data collection systems improve, and more detailed and accurate input data is collected by insurers (and agents and brokers), such that the granularity of the details of the risks improves, modeling can be expected to become an even more effective underwriting tool. Long term, this should lead to better risk management and more capacity in geographic areas where current capacity may be more limited by the lack of use of these tools. One would also expect capacity to expand as more insurers utilize these risk management approaches.[36]

As noted above, rating agencies, such as A.M. Best, are monitoring insurance companies' use of modeling in managing exposure. In addition, since the 2005 hurricane season, rating agencies are now more focused on insurers' accumulations with regard to all perils, not just terrorism.[37] The greater attention by rating agencies and other private market participants regarding accumulations and the use of models will likely increase the number of insurers using accumulation exposure and deterministic modeling going forward.

Conclusion

The amount of capital an insurance company is willing to allocate to a particular risk, line, or region, is based largely on its understanding of its maximum loss under different scenarios. To that end, insurers have made greater use of sophisticated modeling of severities of terrorism events to measure and manage accumulations of risk in any given location or area. Improved risk accumulation management allows insurers to diversify and control their terrorism risk exposures, and may encourage additional capacity in the long term. As the tools insurers use continue to evolve and improve, it is reasonable to expect terrorism risk insurance to become more available.

B.2. Modeling Terrorist Attacks

Developments in Probabilistic Modeling

In addition to the approaches discussed in section B.1, probabilistic models are also used by insurance companies to evaluate and manage risk exposure. These models not only estimate the severity of an event (amount of insured losses), but the frequency of an event (how often, where, and what type). Unlike the models described in section B.1 that broadly estimate the severity of risk exposure, probabilistic models focus on the loss potential under various scenarios (*e.g.*, the likelihood or probability of an attack at a given target, using a specific mode of attack, over a certain period of time). The models are used to develop loss probability distributions, also called loss exceedence curves.

---

[36] The American Insurance Association also noted that availability of capacity will remain in accord with sound risk management practices, driven largely by accumulation management. American Insurance Association, Comments to the PWG dated April 21, 2006.

[37] Aon Corporation, Comments to the PWG dated April 21, 2006; American Academy of Actuaries' Terrorism Risk Insurance Subgroup, Comments to the PWG dated April 21, 2006; Standard & Poor's, "Updated Process To Provide Better Information for Evaluation (Re)Insurers Terrorism Exposure," RatingsDirect, June 8, 2006.

Unlike probabilistic modeling of natural disasters based on historical data and scientific research, there have been few terrorism incidents in the U.S. upon which to perform actuarial analysis in modeling terrorism frequency. In addition, terrorism is an intentional, man-made peril with inherent uncertainties. To compensate, modelers use data from the Department of State, Federal Bureau of Investigation, and other sources which provide information on attacks, prevented attempts, weapons, and terrorist groups. In addition to this historical data, modeling firms use counter-intelligence experts (many with intelligence backgrounds) who specialize in terrorism threat assessment. Various methodologies are used to determine the probabilities of attack; examples include methods based on game theory that parameterize terrorist strategic behavior and adaptive response to deterrence, and the Delphi method (developed by the RAND Corporation during World War II), in which expert opinions are statistically combined into probability distributions.

Probabilistic models continue to evolve and extend the ability to analyze possible targets and attack modes. Under the current state of modeling practice, probabilistic models are updated annually for changes in risk assessment. Finding a viable way to share government intelligence with modelers and their experts has been suggested as a way to improve terrorism modeling.[38] Over time, probabilistic models are expected to continue to evolve as knowledge and experience grows.

Skeptical of their reliability, insurers do not appear to be placing much weight on the probabilistic models at this time. A.M. Best reports that among surveyed insurers, only 19 percent reported using probabilistic modeling while 62 percent did not.[39] As the NAIC pointed out during consultations, the ability to model frequency is uncertain and untested, and some regulators have even challenged advisory organization loss cost filings based on such models. While insurers and reinsurers are willing to allocate some capacity to terrorism risk with untested probability models or by making their own internal probability assessments, given the degree of uncertainty associated with these modeling efforts, there may be limits in the confidence insurers may place on such models. Many commenters (*e.g.*, the Reinsurance Association of America) highlighted the fact that allocating additional capacity is tied to determining potential frequency and severity. Marsh, a leading risk and insurance services firm, explains that terrorism modeling is still in its infancy, but that insurers, reinsurers, and modeling firms are learning more each day.[40] If the ability of insurers to better judge frequency and severity improve as the models continue to develop over time, and as insurers' confidence grows and they begin to use them, it is reasonable to expect terrorism insurance to become more available as capacity grows.

---

[38] Peter Ulrich, Testimony before the Intelligence, Information Sharing, and Terrorism Risk Assessment Subcommittee of the Committee on Homeland Security and the Oversight and Investigations Subcommittee of the Committee on Financial Services of the House of Representatives, U.S. House of Representatives, "Terrorism Threats and the Insurance Market," July 25, 2006.

[39] A.M. Best, Special Report, "Terrorism: Too Risky Without TRIA?," December 2005.

[40] Marsh Inc., Research Report, "Marketwatch: Terrorism Insurance 2006."

Conclusion

An understanding of the potential frequency and severity of terrorist attacks is important for insurers to properly evaluate their risk exposure. Improvements in modeling frequency of terrorist attacks have likely had positive impact on insurers' willingness to provide coverage for terrorism. As further improvements occur over time, it is reasonable to expect further positive impact on market development. However, unlike other catastrophic exposures (*e.g.*, natural disasters) where there are more refined methods of modeling frequency, modeling the frequency of terrorism risk relies largely on analysis of terrorist behavior. Given the nature of these modeling efforts and the uncertainty attached to these probability estimates, the degree of confidence insurers will place in these modeling efforts in evaluating their risk exposures is difficult to evaluate.

B.3. Reinsurance

More Reinsurance Capacity Continues to Be Allocated to Terrorism Risk

Reinsurance plays an important role in the availability of terrorism risk insurance. If direct insurers are able to transfer terrorism risk to others (such as reinsurers), the amount of capital otherwise tied to that risk is then available to issue more policies (see section B.4). Capacity increases when reinsurance markets are available and when insurers access those markets.

Reinsurance for terrorism risk all but vanished on September 11, as reinsurers withdrew from the market. The reinsurance market for terrorism risk insurance, which functions independent of TRIA (which does not cover reinsurance losses), appears to be following a basic pattern of insurance market behavior typically observed after any large insurance catastrophe.[41] As discussed earlier in this report, following a large catastrophe, insurers and reinsurers typically react by reevaluating their portfolios and risk exposures, often declining to renew or issue new policies until the company's exposure and appetite for risk is re-assessed. During this period of re-evaluation, the supply of insurance is generally restricted and prices rise for the more limited capacity that is still available. On the demand side, in many cases demand for coverage increases as policyholders re-assess their individual exposure and coverage. Increased demand and increased prices (and potential returns) attract new capital, both from existing and new market participants. Eventually, insurers and reinsurers re-commit capacity, although it may be re-distributed in some manner as the result of their re-assessment of risk exposures. The reinsurance market has generally followed this trend as there has been some return of private reinsurance market capacity in the 5 years after September 11.

---

[41] David Cummins, "Should the Government Provide Insurance for Catastrophes?" Federal Reserve Bank of St. Louis *REVIEW* (July/August 2006); U.S. Department of Treasury, Report to Congress, "Assessment: The Terrorism Risk Insurance Act of 2002," (June 30, 2005), p. 27, noting that market behavior following the September 11 attacks was generally consistent with the beginning stages of an underwriting or loss cycle typical in response to a catastrophic loss shock.

Data on reinsurance capacity for terrorism risk is limited to surveys and estimates of trade groups, brokers, and industry participants. Perhaps the most commonly cited source is a survey of reinsurance brokers and underwriters by the Reinsurance Association of America (RAA). The RAA estimates that currently the global reinsurance capacity available in the U.S. for terrorism risk *at current market conditions* is between $6-$8 billion.[42] The RAA's most recent estimates indicate an increase from the approximate $4-$6 billion in terrorism risk reinsurance capacity that was available in 2005.[43] An important point in interpreting these estimates is that they are constructed at current market conditions, which indicates reinsurers' willingness to provide capacity at current market prices. These estimates would not appear to reflect the willingness of reinsurers to make capacity available under different market conditions.

Other industry participants broadly agree with the RAA's evaluation of currently available reinsurance capacity for terrorism risk. Swiss Re, a top global reinsurer, and Aon Corporation (Aon), a leading risk management service provider and insurance and reinsurance broker, reported to the PWG that the total private reinsurance market capacity for terrorism risk is in the range of $6-$8 billion today.[44] This capacity is available for conventional terrorism risks. The RAA, Swiss Re, and Aon estimate that apart from the $6-$8 billion of available reinsurance, another $900 million to $1.6 billion of reinsurance capacity is available and is being used to reinsure CNBR terrorism risks.[45]

In addition to the $6-$8 billion in capacity from traditional reinsurers, some terrorism risk capacity may be emerging from capital market participants. It was reported to the PWG that hedge funds and other investors have some capacity available for terrorism risk. Aon estimates the potential capital of hedge funds and other investors to be in the range of around $2-$3 billion (*albeit* at prices generally higher than traditional reinsurers charge).[46] The RAA, in reporting on its survey of reinsurers and brokers, stated that it estimates potential hedge fund capacity to currently be approximately $3-$4 billion.[47]

---

[42] Reinsurance Association of America, Comments to the PWG dated April 21, 2006. The RAA's estimate is developed by contacting key reinsurance providers to determine what capacity is available. Their estimate includes both standalone and multi-peril treaty reinsurance. Reinsurance Association of America, Comments to the PWG dated April 21, 2006.

[43] Franklin W. Nutter (President, Reinsurance Association of America (RAA)), Testimony before the Committee on Banking, Housing and Urban Affairs, U.S. Senate, "Oversight of the Terrorism Risk Insurance Program," April 14, 2005; American Insurance Association, Comments to the PWG dated April 21, 2006, citing an estimated $4 to $6 billion in reinsurance capacity during 2005; Wharton Risk Management and Decision Processes Center, "TRIA and Beyond," The Wharton School, University of Pennsylvania, August 2005, estimating 2005 reinsurance capacity at $5 to $6 billion based on its own survey.

[44] Swiss Re, Comments to the PWG dated April 20, 2006; Aon Corporation, Comments to the PWG dated April 21, 2006.

[45] Reinsurance Association of America, Comments to the PWG dated April 21, 2006; Swiss Re, Comments to the PWG dated April 20, 2006; Aon Corporation, Comments to the PWG dated April 21, 2006.

[46] Aon Corporation, Comments to the PWG dated April 21, 2006.

[47] Reinsurance Association of America, Comments to the PWG dated April 21, 2006. The RAA's comment on potential hedge fund capacity was qualified, however, as it questions whether any transactions accessing this potential capacity will develop.

Capital market instruments, such as catastrophe bonds, also provide a potential mechanism for transferring terrorism risk to capital market investors. Approximately $1.9 billion in natural catastrophe bond transactions that took place during 2005[48], and all insurance-linked debt outstanding reportedly totals about $20 billion.[49] Current levels of capital market participation in insurance-linked transactions represent a small fraction of the capital available to hedge funds and other capital market investors. Whether capital enters the market through catastrophe bonds, insurance swaps, or, more directly through financially-backed offshore reinsurance vehicles, capital market investors present a potential capital source. However, there are often cited potential limits to greater capital market participation in the market for terrorism risk reinsurance, even in comparison to natural catastrophe reinsurance. In general, some investors may be attracted to natural catastrophe exposures because such exposures my not be correlated with general market conditions. In contrast, a large-scale terrorist attack may be positively correlated with overall market conditions – and such uncertainty (given limited experience) may limit the desirability of such investments for some capital market participants. However, capital market investors are attracted to potentially higher returns. Long term, more capital market capacity may emerge if insurers become more willing to pay higher prices for such reinsurance.[50]

It is important to remember that all of these estimates are of reinsurers' willingness and capital market interest to provide capacity at current market prices. These estimates do not reflect estimates of capacity that may become available under different market conditions.[51]

Currently, Insurers Do Not Appear Willing to Purchase Much Reinsurance Which Affects Capacity Even at Current Market Conditions

The amount of reinsurance capacity allocated for terrorism risk also depends on the willingness of insurers to purchase coverage. Much like the decision of individual policyholders on how much insurance to purchase, insurers make a similar decision regarding reinsurance that is based on their perception of risk, price of coverage, and ability to manage risk.

The 2005 Treasury study found that the share of insurers purchasing some reinsurance for certified acts of terrorism dropped from 70 percent in 2003 to 65 percent

---

[48] Franklin W. Nutter, (President, Reinsurance Association of America), Testimony before the Terrorism Insurance Implementation Working Group, National Association of Insurance Commissioners, March 29, 2006.

[49] Swiss Re, Comments to the PWG dated April 20, 2006.

[50] It is not clear that what form capital market capacity may take. Some question whether it will be through catastrophe bonds, citing rating agency failure to rate the instruments and the correlation to other sector disruptions. See Reinsurance Association of America, Comments to the PWG dated April 21, 2006. What is important, however, is the reported development of capital market capacity rather than the particular mechanism, whether through bonds or newly-formed, investor-backed reinsurance entities.

[51] Based on PWG consultations with reinsurer groups.

in 2004, but rose to 75 percent in early 2005.[52] Similarly, A.M. Best's 2004 surveys revealed that 59 percent of insurers purchased private reinsurance for their terrorism risk retention while 38 percent did not purchase any reinsurance, and 3 percent did not respond to the question.[53]

Examining reinsurance purchase by broad lines, Treasury found that a fairly consistent percentage of insurers did not buy any reinsurance for their TRIA retention: over 30 percent of insurers writing property coverage in 2004, more than 20 percent of insurers writing liability policies, and between 20 and 30 percent of insurers writing workers' compensation programs. Workers' compensation was the only area between 2003 and 2004 where more reinsurance was purchased. A.M. Best's 2004 surveys found that 83 percent of those that did purchase reinsurance were medium and large insurers.[54] The Treasury study found that large insurers reinsured a much smaller percentage of their exposure in TRIA-covered lines than did small and medium insurers.[55] This last result is probably due to greater diversification of large insurers.

Reasons why insurers do not purchase more reinsurance coverage for terrorism risk insurance (even at modest amounts) are difficult to pinpoint conclusively, but it appears that pricing and comfort with their own risk exposures are factors. Based on a 2005 survey, Moody's reported that "[a]lmost universally, companies are not purchasing private reinsurance specifically for terrorism losses in the TRIA retention layer." The surveyed insurers said that while this coverage was available, they were not using it because it was priced too high. Most insurers are obtaining some reinsurance coverage from private reinsurers for terrorism losses under their property reinsurance or casualty treaties. However, Moody's concluded that: "Consistent with our 2003 survey, Moody's would still characterize the proportion of terrorism risk being shifted from primary insurers to private market reinsurers as low."[56] As discussed below, TRIA appears to have had a negative impact on the demand for reinsurance.

Marsh reported in its most recent 2006 Marketwatch report that the main reasons insurers were not buying reinsurance were: cost; adequate coverage in existing reinsurance treaties; the inability to pass on reinsurance costs to policyholders; limited

---

[52] U.S. Department of Treasury, Report to Congress, "Assessment: The Terrorism Risk Insurance Act of 2002," (June 30, 2005), pp. 5, 112-113.

[53] A.M. Best, Special Report, "Terrorism: Too Risky Without TRIA?," December 2005.

[54] A.M. Best, *Ibid.*

[55] U.S. Department of Treasury, Report to Congress, "Assessment: The Terrorism Risk Insurance Act of 2002," (June 30, 2005), pp. 114-120. The definitions of "large" and "small" insurers used in the A.M. Best and Treasury studies are not directly comparable. The Treasury study defines insurer size classes in terms of total assets, while the A.M. Best's survey defines insurer size classes in terms of total surplus. An approximate method used to translate surplus into the corresponding value of total assets suggests that all insurers in A.M. Best's small and medium size classes, and some of those considered by A.M. Best to be large insurers, would be categorized as small insurers for the purposes of the Treasury survey. Furthermore the A.M. Best survey question was addressed to a slightly different population of insurers. The size-related results from the Treasury and A.M. Best surveys appear to be compatible once these differences are taken into account.

[56] Moody's Investors Service, Special Comment, "Terrorism Risk Remains Material for Insurers as TRIA Expiration Looms," June 2005.

capacity/limits at affordable rates; better control of aggregate exposures; comfort with their TRIA retentions; and insufficient coverage for CNBR.[57] Aon reports that although the market for terrorism reinsurance has softened since January 2002 and standalone and "all risk" property insurers are able to purchase some coverage, price is still perceived as relatively high and the lack of reinsurance *at affordable prices* has deterred new market entrants. In addition, Aon points to Berkshire Hathaway as a source of "considerable available capacity," but that insurers have found the pricing too high.[58]

Long Term, Additional Terrorism Reinsurance Capacity Depends on Improved Modeling and the Willingness of Insurers to Pay Higher Prices

Reinsurers decide how to allocate their capital, both between U.S. and non-U.S. markets, within the U.S. market, and among the types of insurance to be reinsured (*e.g.*, between natural disasters and terrorism risk). Some reinsurers also issue primary insurance through affiliates and, as a result, allocate capacity between reinsurance and primary terrorism risk insurance. Pricing (a function largely of demand), loss experience, and the ability to predict frequency of loss are among the key determinants in reinsurers' capital allocation decisions and the willingness of other capital providers (*e.g.*, through catastrophe bonds) to allocate capital to terrorism risk.[59] As Swiss Re noted in comments to the PWG, new capital is allocated where potential return on capital is substantial and secure in terms of being able to project expected losses.[60] When severity and variations are difficult to quantify, such as with terrorism risk, the return on capital needs to be higher in light of the uncertain and potentially large risk exposure.

Marsh reports that reinsurers put limited capital at risk for terrorism exposures, given their lack of confidence in how to underwrite, model, or price for this peril.[61] It is not clear to what extent reinsurers are modeling terrorism risk. In December 2005, A.M. Best reported that very few reinsurers responded to its SRQ's questions about aggregation risk exposure.[62] Based on consultations with reinsurers and the comments received, reinsurers – like primary insurers – are using accumulation models (together with standalone reinsurance contracts) and are relying less on probabilistic models. Overall, the RAA reports that improved techniques of understanding and managing these exposures have encouraged some additional incremental capacity in the reinsurance market. The RAA states that not much additional improvement can be expected, however, largely because reinsurers continue to have difficulty estimating the expected frequency of events.[63]

---

[57] Marsh Inc., Research Report, "Marketwatch: Terrorism Insurance 2006."
[58] Aon Corporation, Comments to the PWG dated April 21, 2006.
[59] Swiss Re, Comments to the PWG dated April 20, 2006. Swiss Re explained that in making pricing and capacity allocation decisions, reinsurers consider: experience with the risk such that frequency and severity of expected losses can be projected, including variations from norms; sufficient economic incentives (*i.e.*, return on capital); and the ability to limit exposure.
[60] Swiss Re, *Ibid.*
[61] Marsh Inc., Research Report, "Marketwatch: Terrorism Insurance 2006."
[62] A.M. Best, Special Report, "Terrorism: Too Risky Without TRIA?," December 2005.
[63] Reinsurance Association of America, Comments to the PWG dated April 21, 2006.

Reinsurers do have the ability to limit their overall exposure through the terms of reinsurance contracts. In order to establish their capacity for terrorism risk reinsurance, underwriters generally evaluate their surplus position to determine an amount of capital that they can reasonably put at risk to cover terrorism exposure. Then they carefully underwrite to manage aggregate exposure to potential terrorism loss events within the established limits.[64] One way reinsurers manage this exposure is by putting the capital they will offer into standalone contracts.[65] In this way, reinsurers can assess and manage their terrorism exposures on a contract-by-contract, individual risk-by-risk basis, rather than by reinsuring an entire portfolio of policies (*e.g.*, reinsurance treaties) without a clear appreciation of the total exposure. For workers' compensation, terrorism coverage is generally placed within their overall catastrophe programs. Some regional insurers with exposures outside cities and business centers secure coverage in their standard reinsurance programs usually with some limitations.[66]

The challenges in quantifying potential losses from acts of terrorism (see section B.2) and a general reluctance of insurers to pay higher prices for terrorism risk insurance have a negative impact on the amount of capacity reinsurers are willing to provide.[67] For example, several stakeholders pointed to Berkshire Hathaway (National Indemnity) as having considerable available capacity, yet it is almost always prefaced with the explanation that Berkshire Hathaway requires a price that many direct insurers find too high.[68] During consultations, reinsurers explained that a willingness by insurers to purchase reinsurance at a sufficient price would attract some additional capacity into the market. Swiss Re believes that capacity will not substantially increase in the foreseeable future due to a number of challenges, including low market penetration and insufficient returns to reinsurers (especially in light of the uncertainties in predicting frequency).[69] In comments to the PWG, Liberty Mutual explained it this way:

> There is an inverse relationship between availability and affordability. In order to increase availability, we need to attract new capital. In order to attract new capital, we need to provide investors a return on that capital commensurate with the risk that they may lose that capital. Such new capital may be available at a price that customers are not willing to pay.[70]

The presence of subsidized Federal reinsurance through TRIA appears to negatively affects the emergence of private reinsurance capacity because it dilutes demand for private sector reinsurance.[71] The Lloyd's of London market commented that TRIA appears to have a negative influence on some demand for reinsurance and that it is possible that the withdrawal of TRIA after 2007 will encourage the development of some

---

[64] Reinsurance Association of America, *Ibid.*

[65] Marsh Inc., Comment to the PWG dated April 20, 2006; Reinsurance Association of America, *Ibid.*

[66] Reinsurance Association of America, *Ibid.*

[67] See generally, Swiss Re, Comments to the PWG dated April 20, 2006.

[68] Aon Corporation, Comments to the PWG dated April 21, 2006.

[69] Swiss Re, Comments to the PWG dated April 20, 2006.

[70] Liberty Mutual Group, Comments to the PWG dated April 21, 2006.

[71] See generally, U.S. Department of Treasury, Report to Congress, "Assessment: The Terrorism Risk Insurance Act of 2002," (June 30, 2005).

limited private market solutions, especially in a favorable claims environment; however, significant growth to the point at which reinsurance is generally available at prices that insurers are prepared to pay appears questionable, in Lloyd's view.[72] In early 2005, the Wharton Risk Center collaborated with two leading insurance company trade groups in surveying 40 member companies, 10 of which responded to the question: "How much reinsurance would your company want to purchase if TRIA is not renewed?" Not one insurer said it would buy less reinsurance; 9 insurers indicated that they would purchase more reinsurance, while 1 insurer said it would maintain the same level of reinsurance.[73] As estimates of current reinsurance capacity reflect current market conditions, they do not appear to reflect the willingness of reinsurers to supply more capacity under different market conditions.

Conclusion

The terrorism risk reinsurance market has improved since the aftermath of September 11. Reinsurers have gradually allocated more capital to the terrorism risk due to improvements in the market (better understanding and modeling of the risk, primary insurers' management of accumulations, favorable loss experience, and pricing), and available capacity continues to increase year to year. Long term, if insurers were willing to pay higher reinsurance costs and were willing to pass along those costs to policyholders, additional reinsurance capacity would likely enter the market and alternative risk transfer mechanisms might develop. Like other markets, the supply curve for reinsurance is generally upward sloping (quantity supplied increases with price). However, even with improvements in pricing, given the nature of evaluating the probability of loss through models, it is difficult to speculate on the amount of reinsurance capacity or capital from other sources that may be available for terrorism risk.

B.4. Terrorism Risk Insurance Market

Policyholder Surplus and Available Capital Have Increased

The amount of terrorism risk insurance an insurance company may be willing to provide is based on its "book of business" (types of insurance, locations, *etc.*), appetite for risk, use of reinsurance, available capital, and (as noted in sections B.1 and B.2), its ability to understand risk exposures. A key determinant in how much risk an insurer is willing to assume is the strength of its capital. Property and casualty insurers maintain a certain amount of capital in order to underwrite a certain level of risk, with the amounts of capital determined by a combination of state insurance regulations, rating agency requirements, and an insurer's own tolerance for risk. As with other businesses, the capital of insurance companies is measured by net worth (its assets less its liabilities), and

---

[72] Lloyd's of London, Comments to the PWG dated April 21, 2006.
[73] Wharton Risk Management and Decision Processes Center, "TRIA and Beyond," The Wharton School, University of Pennsylvania, August 2005.

it is also broadly referred to as "policyholder surplus."[74] Policyholder surplus is generally thought of as the amount of capital an insurer keeps to cover the claims and expenses expected to come from the policies it issues. The amount of capital maintained by insurance companies is also often referred to as "capacity" in that it dictates the amount of insurance the insurer is able to issue.[75] Accordingly, capacity to underwrite insurance, including terrorism insurance, is tied to the financial status of the property and casualty industry as a whole, and insurance companies individually. As shown in the table below, policyholder surplus industry-wide has returned and now exceeds pre-September 11 levels.

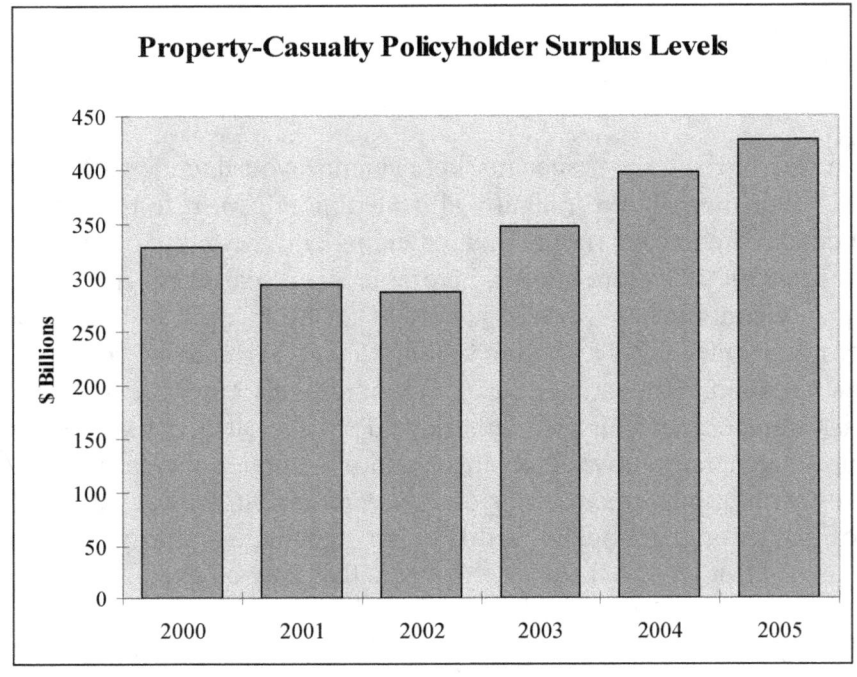

Source: NAIC

As measured by the NAIC, policyholder surplus retained by property and casualty insurers grew from approximately $287.5 billion at year end 2002 to $427 billion at year-end 2005.[76] At the end of first half of 2006, policyholder surplus is estimated by A.M. Best to be $450.5 billion[77], and is projected by Marsh to reach $467.8 billion by year end.[78] The decline in policyholder surplus over 2001 and 2002 was driven in large part by the insured losses from the September 11 terrorist attacks and reduced investment returns. Over time, industry policyholder surplus levels have increased well beyond 2001-2002 levels, even following large natural catastrophe losses in 2005, which were

---

[74] Wharton, *Ibid.*

[75] Financial Services Fact Book 2006, Insurance Information Institute, p. 70.

[76] Information provided by the National Association of Insurance Commissioners. A.M. Best estimated policyholder surplus at $444.5 billion through first quarter 2006, up from its year-end 2005 surplus calculation of $438.7 billion. A.M. Best, Special Report, "First-Quarter 2006 P/C Underwriting Results Improve From Year-End 2005," August 2006.

[77] "U.S. P/C Reports Underwriting Profit in First Half of 2006," *BestWire*, September 15, 2006.

[78] Marsh Inc., "U.S. Insurance Market Report Third Quarter 2006," September 2006, p. 5.

more than offset by investment returns and industry profits.[79] As Treasury pointed out in its 2005 study (and as discussed earlier in this report), the dip in surplus in 2001 and 2002 followed by increases in the subsequent years reflect the typical insurance market response following a large catastrophic event. Initial losses negatively affect surplus levels, which limits the supply of insurance and increases prices.[80] Higher prices rebuild surplus, attract new capital, increase capacity and the insurance supply, and prices begin to fall. As the data below suggest, in terms of the long-term availability and affordability of terrorism insurance going forward, the effects of the September 11 losses on the financial capabilities of the industry are no longer a factor. Other factors discussed in this report, however, remain.

Policyholder surplus generally increases as insurance company profits increase, and some portion of the increase in policyholder surplus should be related to profits earned on providing terrorism risk insurance (for those that charged premiums for the coverage). This is especially true as there have been no claims for terrorism losses in the U.S. to offset premium collections. The 2005 Treasury report estimated that based on NAIC and survey data, terrorism insurance premiums, excluding workers' compensation, were roughly $700 million in 2002, $2.3 billion in 2003 and $2.7 billion in 2004.[81] Based on a more limited sample, A.M. Best reported that the amount of terrorism premiums, including workers' compensation, received during 2004 by 155 insurers responding to their SRQ was $1.097 billion, and that from that about $800 million in annual after-tax terrorism premiums had been added to surplus. Even applying A.M. Best's conservative figure, assuming this to have been roughly constant and representing the industry as a whole, the industry increased policyholder surplus by a total of approximately $1.7 billion during 2002 through 2004, as a result of premiums for terrorism.[82] Based on the 2005 Treasury study and A.M. Best's survey, it appears that somewhere in the range of $3-$8 billion in terrorism risk insurance premiums have been collected through 2005, and a significant portion of these premiums should have accrued to policyholder surplus. In addition, premiums that accrue to policyholder surplus also grow over time with an insurance company's investment returns, which should further increase direct capacity available to underwrite terrorism risk in excess of the approximate $3-$8 billion in collected terrorism risk insurance premiums. By way of comparison, the RAA estimates that the total aggregate reinsurance market capacity was approximately $4-$6 billion last year and is approximately $6-$8 currently (see section B.3).

---

[79] A.M. Best, Special Report, "U.S. P/C Industry Reports Operating Profit in 2005 Despite Record-High Catastrophe Losses," May 2006.
[80] U.S. Department of Treasury, Report to Congress, "Assessment: The Terrorism Risk Insurance Act of 2002," (June 30, 2005), p. 15.
[81] U.S. Department of Treasury, *Ibid.*, p. 63.
[82] A.M. Best, Special Report, "Terrorism: Too Risky Without TRIA?," December 2005.

Insurer Retentions Have Increased Under TRIA

Over the same post-September 11 period in which the property and casualty industry's financial health improved, insurer retentions under the TRIA Program have increased.

As discussed in section I.A, each insurance company participating in the TRIA Program first retains a certain aggregate amount of any claims covered by the terrorism risk insurance policies it issues before becoming eligible for Federal reinsurance payments under the TRIA Program. Once that threshold amount of paid claims, or deductible, is met, the insurance company pays 10 percent (in 2006) and 15 percent (in 2007) of additional losses, and the TRIA Program pays the rest (not exceeding the $100 billion aggregate insured loss cap).

An insurer's TRIA deductible remains constant no matter how much terrorism risk insurance coverage it sells because the deductible base is the previous year's sales of commercial property and casualty insurance, not just terrorism insurance.[83] Thus, each insurer has *at least* that much capital, up to its own deductible, that could potentially be exposed to terrorism risk insurance losses. Still, each insurance company decides how much of its capital to allocate to terrorism risk knowing that below its TRIA deductible it will be responsible for the losses without the help of the Federal government. The amount of policyholder surplus and the availability of reinsurance factor into such decisions.

The insurer's deductible has gradually increased through the life of the 5-year TRIA Program. The insurer deductible, as a percentage of the prior year's direct earned premiums, has risen from 7 percent in 2003, to 10 percent in 2004, 15 percent in 2005, 17.5 percent in 2006, and 20 percent in 2007.

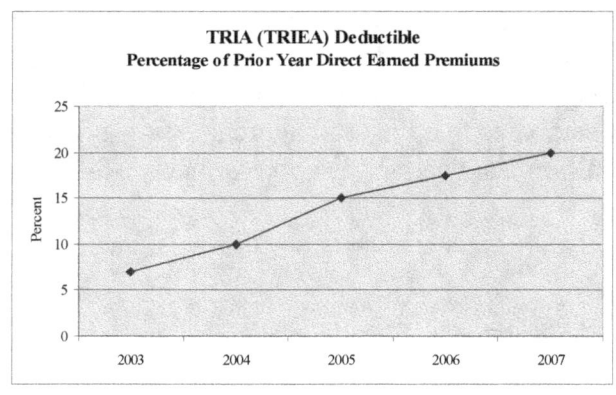

---

[83] Commercial property and casualty insurance, under TRIA and Treasury's regulations, includes insurance whose premiums are generally reported to state insurance regulators under the following lines of business on the NAIC Annual Statement Exhibit of Premiums and Losses (commonly known as Statutory Page 14): Line 1 – Fire; Line 2.1 – Allied Lines; Line 5.1 – Commercial Multiple Peril (non-liability portion); Line 5.2 – Commercial Multiple Peril (liability portion); Line 8 – Ocean Marine; Line 9 – Inland Marine; Line 16 – Workers' Compensation; Line 17 – Other Liability; Line 18 – Products Liability; Line 22 – Aircraft (all perils); and Line 27 – Boiler and Machinery. 31 C.F.R. §50.5(n).

In addition to the annual increases in the deductible percentage, between 2003 and 2004 industry aggregate direct earned premiums (DEP) also increased (as shown on the table below).[84] Yet although direct earned premium in TRIA lines decreased between 2004 and 2005 as a result of fewer lines or types of insurance remaining in the TRIA Program (see section I.A), the aggregate insurer deductible remained stable at approximately $32 billion in 2005 and $31.8 in 2006, according to data from A.M. Best).[85] As the TRIA deductible increases to 20 percent in 2007, one would expect that the aggregate insurer deductible will likely increase. Assuming direct earned premium from TRIA lines remains constant in 2006, the 2007 insurer deductible would be about $36.4 billion.

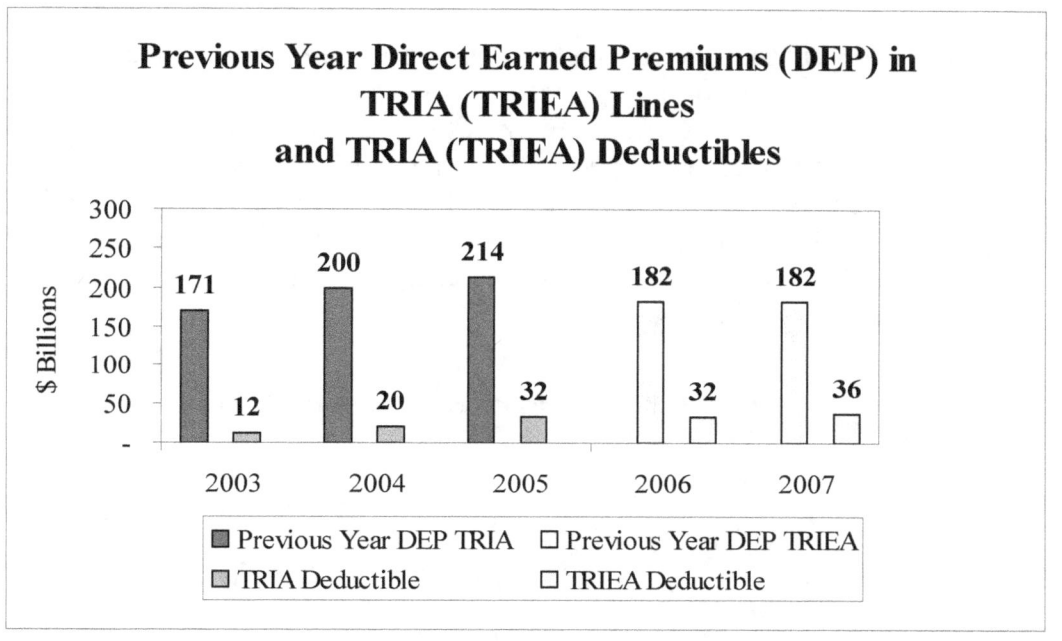

Source: A.M. Best

Terrorism Risk Insurance Premiums Have Declined or Remained Relatively Stable

Approaches used by insurers to quote prices on terrorism insurance vary. Some insurers use loss costs determined by insurance rating bureaus, nominal policy surcharges, or, as discussed in section B.6, provide the coverage for free. Terrorism risk insurance is also priced as a percentage applied against insured value, called "Rate Against Total Insured Value"; a percentage of the overall property premium; a percentage applied against the loss limit offered in the policy, called "Rate on Line"; or a fixed dollar

---

[84] Although each insurance company's deductible is calculated individually, measuring the industry's aggregate deductible provides a rough measure of overall exposure under the assumption of a proportionate spreading of losses among all insurers from a terrorist event.

[85] The direct earned premium for 2005 includes premium for professional liability, which is not covered under TRIA, because its premium is reported for premium reporting purposes as "other liability", which is a line otherwise covered under TRIA. Professional liability is not a separate premium reported line so the aggregate premium may be overstated somewhat.

amount of premium per million of coverage ("$X per $X million of loss limit").[86] Regardless of what approach each insurer employs, the most common measures used for evaluating pricing on terrorism risk insurance are terrorism risk insurance premiums as a percentage against total insured value and as a percentage of overall property insurance premiums. These measures demonstrate the general trends since the passage of TRIA are of declining or relatively stable terrorism risk insurance premiums.

Premium as Percent of Overall Premium

A number of sources indicate that terrorism risk insurance premiums measured as a percentage of overall premiums have decreased since the period following September 11.[87] Some specific examples include the following:

- The 2005 Treasury study found that among insurers who charged for terrorism risk insurance the cost as a percentage of overall premium was: 3.7 percent in 2002, 2.4 percent in 2003, and 3.1 percent by 2004. Surveyed policyholders who paid for the coverage reported that it cost 4 percent of premium in 2002, 2.8 percent in 2003, and 2.7 percent in 2004.[88] The Treasury survey of policyholders found that by 2004, terrorism risk insurance cost most policyholders, including those in high-risk cities, less than 3 percent of the overall premiums, including those in high-risk cities.[89]

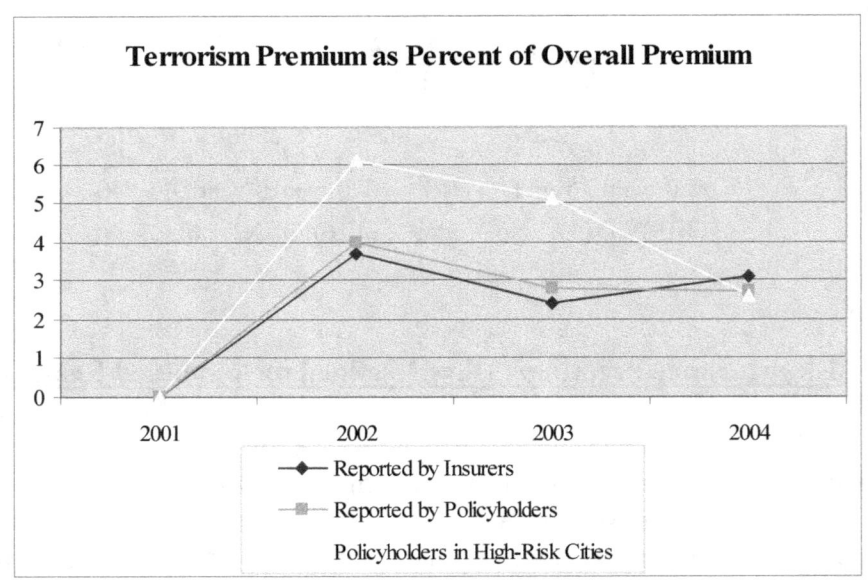

Source: Treasury Department

---

[86] Aon Corporation, Comments to the PWG dated April 21, 2006; Moody's Investors Service, Special Comment, "Terrorism Risk Remains Material for Insurers as TRIA Expiration Looms," June 2005.

[87] See for example, Marsh Inc., Research Report, "Marketwatch: Terrorism Insurance 2006"; Marsh, Inc., "Terrorism 2006 – Year to Date," presentation to PWG staff, July 2006; Marsh Inc., Comments to the PWG dated April 20, 2006; Aon Corporation, Comments to the PWG dated April 21, 2006; Aon Corporation, "Property Terrorism Update – TRIA in the Balance," October 2005.

[88] U.S. Department of Treasury, Report to Congress, "Assessment: The Terrorism Risk Insurance Act of 2002," (June 30, 2005), pp. 4, 64.

[89] U.S. Department of Treasury, Ibid., pp. 86-87.

- Aon reported that in late 2005 that TRIA pricing as a percent of property premium was about 3 percent.[90] While the percentage of premium appears volatile when measured quarter-by-quarter (Aon reports a current spike to about 6 percent in the second quarter 2006 following about 3 percent in the first quarter), over time the percentage has been mostly in the 3 to 5 percent range.

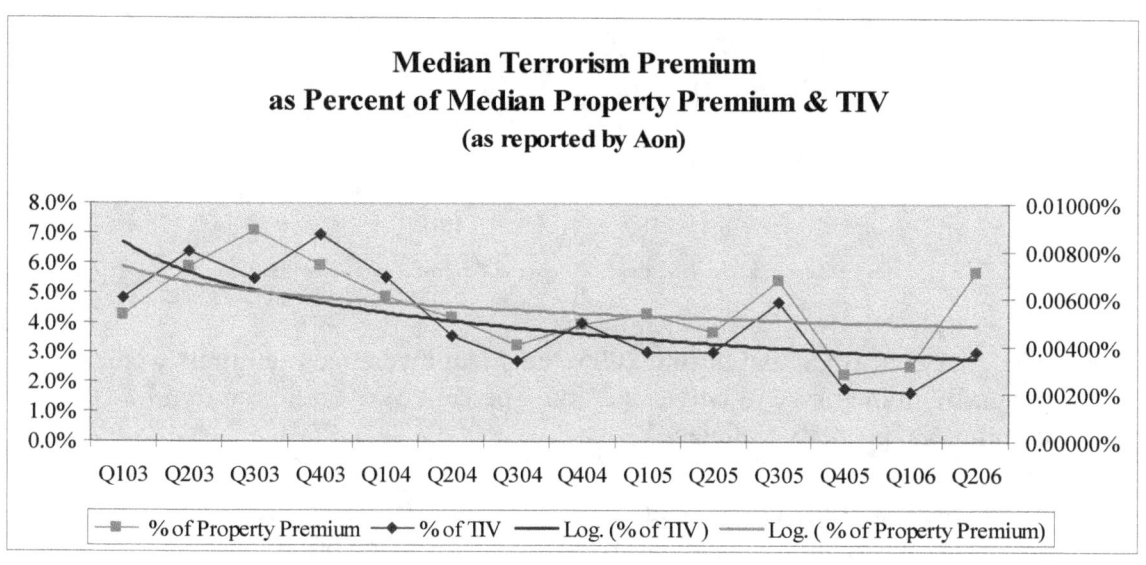

Source: Aon

- Marsh recently reported that there was a moderate reduction in the median percentage of a company's annual property program costs attributable to terrorism premiums: 4.2 percent in 2005 from 4.7 percent in 2004[91], and from the median percentage of 4.4 percent in 2003.[92] Marsh also did a snapshot of terrorism risk insurance pricing in 2006 that showed similar trends but higher rates.[93]

---

[90] Aon Corporation, "Property Terrorism Update – TRIA in the Balance," October 2005.

[91] Marsh Inc., Research Report, "Marketwatch: Terrorism Insurance 2006."

[92] Marsh, Inc., Research Report, "Marketwatch: Terrorism Insurance 2005." See also, Marsh, Inc., Research Report, "Marketwatch: Property Terrorism Insurance 2004," reporting a median of 4.36 percent during three quarters of 2003.

[93] Marsh's snapshot of early 2006 shows that terrorism pricing as a percentage of property premiums also continued to drop in early 2006, although based on a revised 2005 percent of 4.7 percent based on a sampling of roughly 400+ accounts. The median terrorism premium as a percent of property premium among a sample of various accounts from January 1, 2006 to May 1, 2006 is reported as having dropped from 4.7 percent in 2005 to 4.5 in 2006. A sampling of the year to year comparisons of 189 of the same accounts confirmed the trend, though with slightly higher proportional premiums as compared to the wider sample of over 400 accounts, from 5.03 percent in 2005 to 4.92 percent in 2006. Marsh, Inc., "Terrorism 2006 – Year to Date," presentation to PWG staff, July 2006.

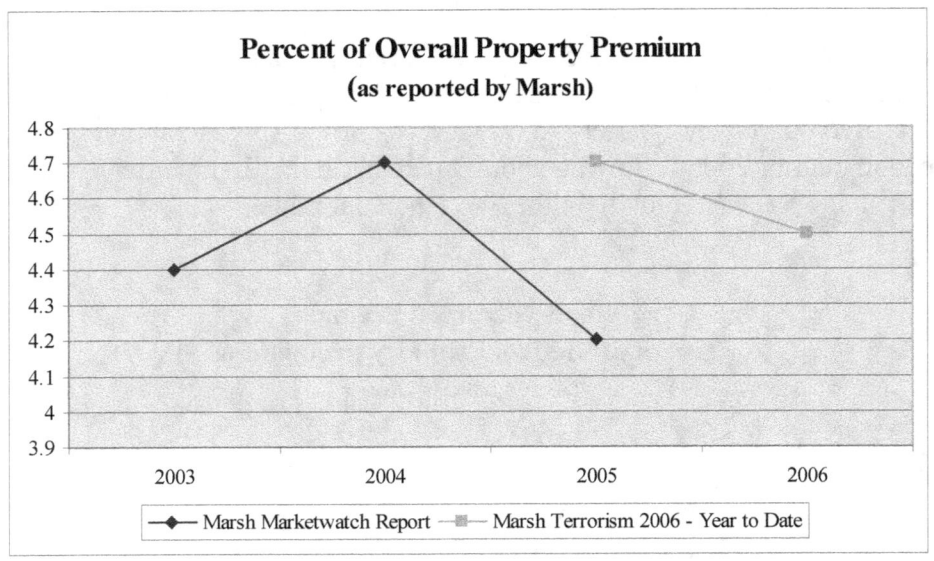

Percent of Overall Property Premium
(as reported by Marsh)

Legend: Marsh Marketwatch Report — Marsh Terrorism 2006 - Year to Date

Source: Marsh

- The AIA confirmed that during 2005, terrorism insurance premiums were generally in the range of between 2 and 4 percent of overall premium for commercial property policies.[94]

- Marsh also examined percentage cost by 15 industry categories. The general pattern shows relatively stable terrorism risk insurance pricing across most industry categories, with larger percent increases in the financial institution sector, and larger decreases in the energy and hospitality sectors. The percentage cost also ranged from as high as 9.5 percent for financial institutions to at or below 3 percent for the manufacturing, food and beverage, and retail sectors, as the chart below demonstrates.[95]

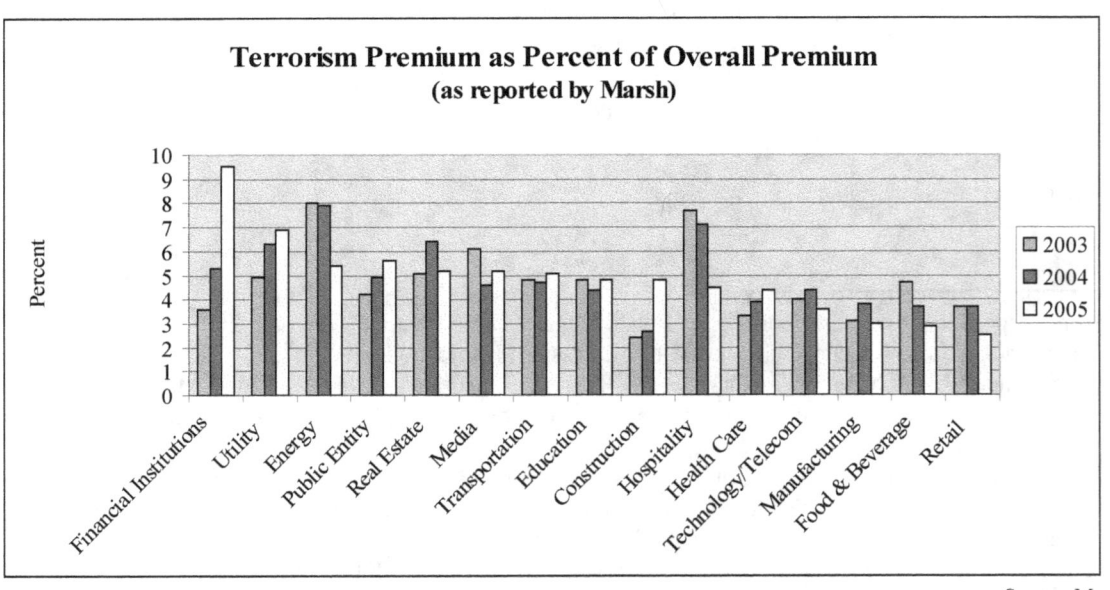

Terrorism Premium as Percent of Overall Premium
(as reported by Marsh)

Source: Marsh

---

[94] American Insurance Association, Comments to the PWG dated April 21, 2006.
[95] Marsh, Inc., Research Report "Marketwatch: Terrorism Insurance 2006."

Premium as Percent of Total Insured Value

A number of sources have compiled data indicating that premiums for terrorism coverage included as part of broader "all risk" property insurance policies and standalone terrorism policies have decreased.[96] Some specific examples include the following:

- Marsh found that premium as a percent against Total Insured Value (or "TIV") for terrorism risk insurance included as part of a broader "all risk" property policies declined (92 percent of their clients/insureds purchase their terrorism coverage as part of property policies).[97] The median percent against TIV fell to 0.0042 percent in 2005 – a 25 percent drop relative to 2004 (0.0057 percent).[98] The percent against TIV had remained unchanged from 2003 to 2004 (0.0057 percent)[99], and during three quarters of 2003, was roughly the same at 0.0056 percent.[100]

- Marsh found that terrorism premiums as a percent against TIV have continued to drop in early 2006. In a follow-up survey, Marsh found that the median rate among 450-484 surveyed accounts from January 1, 2006 to May 1, 2006 remained stable from 0.0046 in 2005 to 0.0045 in 2006 though overall the median premium increased from $12,500 to $13,145. A fixed sample of 189 accounts showed larger decreases in premiums as a percent of TIV between 2005 and 2006. Median terrorism rates dropped from 0.0044 percent in 2005 to 0.0038 percent in 2006.[101]

- According to surveys by the Council of Insurance Agents & Brokers, in the second quarter of 2006 more policyholders were either seeing no change or a decline in terrorism premiums as a percent against TIV – 68 percent. This was up from 60 percent who, in the 1st quarter, reported seeing no change or a decline from the 4th quarter of 2005.[102]

---

[96] See for example, Marsh, Inc., Research Report, "Marketwatch: Terrorism Insurance 2006"; Marsh, Inc., "Terrorism 2006 – Year to Date," presentation to PWG staff, July 2006; Marsh Inc., Comments to the PWG dated April 20, 2006; Aon Corporation, Comments to the PWG dated April 21, 2006; Aon Corporation, "Property Terrorism Update – TRIA in the Balance," October 2005.

[97] Marsh, Inc., Research Report, "Marketwatch: Terrorism Insurance 2006."

[98] Marsh, Inc., *Ibid.*

[99] Marsh, Inc., Research Report, "Marketwatch: Terrorism Insurance 2005."

[100] Marsh, Inc., Research Report, "Marketwatch: Property Terrorism Insurance 2004."

[101] Marsh, Inc., "Terrorism 2006 – Year to Date," presentation to PWG staff, July 2006. The fixed sample's median premiums fell significantly from $37,700 in 2005 to $16,750 in 2006.

[102] The Council of Insurance Agents & Brokers, "Commercial Property/Casualty Market Survey Second Quarter 2006," July 2006; The Council of Insurance Agents & Brokers, "Commercial Property/Casualty Market Survey First Quarter 2006," April 2006. The Council of Insurance Agents & Brokers (CIAB)'s market index survey found that between April and June 2006, terrorism premium as a percent against TIV overall remained fairly steady. Fifty (50) percent reported no change in rates while 18 percent reported a decline in rates, and 9 percent reported an increase (7 percent reported an increase of between 1 to 10 percent). Prior to that, between January and March 2006 terrorism premiums remained fairly steady across

- Marsh reported that the median property terrorism rates decreased between 2004 and 2005, but at slower rates as the size of the company increased.
  - Premiums as a percent against TIV for those companies with TIV less than $100 million decreased more than 55 percent.
  - For companies with TIV between $100 million and $500 million, the median premium as a percent against TIV decreased 22 percent.
  - For companies with TIV between $500 million and $1 billion, the median premium as a percent against TIV decreased 12 percent.
  - For the largest companies – those with TIV more than $1 billion – the median premium as a percent against TIV rate reduction was 6 percent.[103]

- Marsh also reports that median premiums as a percent against TIV decreased for 12 of the 15 industry categories between 2004 and 2005. The 3 industry categories that did not experience declines were Financial Institutions, Utilities, and Education.[104]

- Reports also indicate that premiums as a percent against TIV for terrorism risk insurance sold as a separate standalone policy and not as part of broader property insurance policies, have also decreased.[105] Overall standalone premiums as a percent against TIV declined between 40 and 50 percent since 2002. Risks with locations in capacity "hot spots" (New York City, Chicago, and San Francisco) are an exception, with premiums as a percent against TIV ranging from 0.025 percent to 1 percent on total values.[106]

The above data illustrating general declines or stability in terrorism risk insurance pricing are mostly based on market outcomes observed by brokers and others. Given that many of the policyholders surveyed may be relatively large companies, state insurance regulation may not have played a major role in pricing for these policyholders (see section B.5 for additional details on the interaction of state insurance regulation with terrorism risk insurance). In terms of states or markets where price regulation is more

all regions of the country. Forty-eight (48) percent reported no change, while 19 percent reported a decline, and 12 percent reported an increase (10 percent reported an increase of between 1 to 10 percent).

[103] Marsh, Inc., Research Report, "Marketwatch: Terrorism Insurance 2006."

[104] Marsh, Inc., *Ibid.*

[105] Standalone terrorism insurance provides broad coverage beyond TRIA certified acts coverage and beyond covering U.S. risks. Standalone coverage provides global coverage and includes a broad definition of terrorism. Although there are variations, the most common T3 policy form defines "terrorism" as "An act of terrorism means an act, including the use of force or violence, of any person or group(s) of persons, whether acting alone or on behalf of or in connection with any organization(s), committed for political, religious or ideological purposes including the intention to influence any government and/or to put the public in fear for such purposes." The T3 form excludes NBCR losses. Aon Corporation, "Property Terrorism Update – TRIA in the Balance," October 2005; materials provided by the Lloyd's Market Association. The standalone insurance market both at times competes with "all risk" property insurers that provide TRIA coverage and at other times complements the TRIA coverage. Marsh, Inc., Research Report, "Marketwatch: Terrorism Insurance 2006."

[106] Aon Limited, Aon Crisis Management, "Standalone Terrorism Insurance Market Update," March 2006; Aon Corporation, Comments to the PWG dated April 21, 2006.

prevalent, the general trend since the passage of TRIA has been either stable or slightly higher loss cost approvals.[107]

- Insurance Services Office, Ltd., (ISO)[108] terrorism (certified acts) initial advisory loss costs, as approved by regulators for years 2003 through 2005, with TRIA in place, generally remained steady at $0.03 per $100 of property value in Tier 1 locations (highest risk), $0.018 per $100 in Tier 2 locations (moderate risk); and $0.001 in Tier 3 (low risk).[109] In Tier 1 cities, ISO filed revised loss costs by zip code that distinguished downtown areas. At the end of 2004, ISO developed 4 risk level classifications with ranges as follows: First level (highest-rated) $0.027-$0.075; Second level $0.018-$0.027; Third level $0.009-$0.018; and the Fourth level $0.005-$0.009.[110] Areas are classified by zip code and some locations have been re-assessed (due to modeling of CNBR exposure) and re-classified at different risk levels, which may increase or lower the loss cost used by insurers with their rates.[111]

- In New York, approved terrorism loss cost for building coverage (property only) rose from $0.030 in 2003-2004 to $0.041 in 2005-2006 for Tier 1 locations (Manhattan, 59th Street and below); from $0.018 to 0.021 over that same period for Tier 2 locations (City boroughs), and Tier 3 (the remainder of State) has remained at $0.001 over the same period.[112] In Washington, D.C., approved loss costs for 2005 were $0.075 in high-risk zip code areas and $0.036 in the reminder of the City.[113] These loss costs remain unchanged for 2006.[114]

- National Council on Compensation Insurance, Inc.[115] (NCCI) terrorism loss costs and rates for workers' compensation remained fairly stable.[116] The 2006 median rate is $0.02 per $100 of payroll in the voluntary market (the highest being $0.05

---

[107] "Loss costs" are that part of an insurance rate that cover expected claims and claim adjustment expenses. They are typically filed by insurance advisory organizations with state insurance departments for approval. Generally, once loss costs are approved, insurance companies in the admitted market may use them, adding on to them other expenses (underwriting, *etc.*) and profit, in arriving at its filed rate.

[108] ISO is an insurance advisory organization.

[109] Tier 1 included New York City, San Francisco, Washington, D.C., and Chicago; Tier 2 included Boston, Seattle, Los Angeles, Houston, and Philadelphia; and Tier 3 was the rest of the country.

[110] In the anticipation that TRIA was to expire in December 2005, ISO also prepared higher loss costs, as follows: First level (highest-rated) $0.03-$0.10; Second level $0.02-$0.03; Third level $0.01-$0.02; and the Fourth level $0.005-$0.01.

[111] Information provided by Insurance Services Office, Ltd.

[112] Information provided by the New York State Insurance Department. Figures are for property building coverage only. Other loss costs apply to contents coverage, habitational classes, liability coverage and business owners policies. Also, terrorism premiums in New York are subject to a cap such that terrorism premium cannot exceed 25 percent of the overall policy premium.

[113] Similar to New York, terrorism premiums in the District cannot exceed 25 percent of the overall policy premium.

[114] Information provided by the Office of the Commissioner of the District of Columbia Department of Insurance, Securities and Banking.

[115] NCCI is an insurance advisory organization focused on workers' compensation insurance.

[116] In the involuntary market, NCCI files rates and not loss costs.

in Washington D.C.) and a median rate of $0.03 in the assigned risk market (with a high of $0.07 in D.C.).[117]

Take-Up Rates for Terrorism Coverage Have Increased

The general trend observed throughout the TRIA Program is that more policyholders have been purchasing terrorism risk insurance. Given the general trend of falling or stable prices noted above, an increase in purchases of terrorism risk insurance is not an unexpected outcome. While the typical buyer response to a catastrophe diminishes with time, given recent world events, terrorism insurance demand likely has not fallen as much as is typical.[118] In the current market, take-up rates for terrorism risk insurance have increased and insurance companies have allocated necessary capacity to back the additional coverage sold, despite the modeling difficulties noted in section B.3, the increase in insurer retentions under TRIA, and a generally falling price for terrorism risk insurance.

A number of studies and reports have presented information on policyholder take-up rates. Based on these sources, it appears that in 2002 policyholder take-up was around 30 percent, while today it is around 60 percent.[119] Some examples include the following:

- The 2005 Treasury study found that between 2002 and 2003, take-up increased from 27 percent to 39.5 percent. In 2004, 54 percent of surveyed policyholders reported they had terrorism risk insurance.[120]

- According to Marsh, take-up as of 2005, measured on an annual basis, is 58 percent, up from 49 percent in 2004 and 27 percent in 2003 (including "all risk" property and standalone policies).[121] Marsh has observed similar trends in 2006.[122]

---

[117] Information provided by NCCI.

[118] For a general discussion of buyer behavior, see, Howard Kunreuther and Erwann Michel-Kerjan, "Dealing with Extreme Events: New Challenges for Terrorism Risk Coverage in the U.S.," Center for Risk Management and Decision Processes, The Wharton School, University of Pennsylvania, April 2004, p. 20.

[119] See generally, A.M. Best, Special Report, "Terrorism: Too Risky Without TRIA?," December 2005; Marsh, Inc., Research Report, "Marketwatch: Terrorism Insurance 2006"; Marsh, Inc., "Terrorism 2006 – Year to Date," presentation to PWG staff, July 2006; Marsh, Inc., Comment to the PWG dated April 20, 2006; Aon Corporation, Comments to the PWG dated April 21, 2006; Aon Corporation, "Property Terrorism Update – TRIA in the Balance," October 2005; Moody's Investors Service, Special Comment, "Terrorism Risk Remains Material for Insurers as TRIA Expiration Looms," June 2005; Aon Corporation, "Terrorism Risk Management & Risk Transfer Market Overview," December 2004; Marsh, Inc., Research Report, "Marketwatch: Terrorism Insurance 2005"; Marsh, Inc., Research Report, "Marketwatch: Property Terrorism Insurance 2004."

[120] U.S. Department of Treasury, Report to Congress, "Assessment: The Terrorism Risk Insurance Act of 2002," (June 30, 2005), pp. 3, 84.

[121] Marsh, Inc., Research Report, "Marketwatch: Terrorism Insurance 2006"; Marsh, Inc., Research Report, "Marketwatch: Property Terrorism Insurance 2004"; Marsh, Inc., Comment to the PWG dated April 20, 2006.

[122] Marsh, Inc., "Terrorism 2006 – Year to Date," presentation to PWG staff, July 2006. Of a sample of over 400 insureds, Marsh found take-up increased among the sample population from 49.3 percent in 2005

- Aon similarly found that 59.3 percent of all policyholders purchased some form of property terrorism insurance in 2005, up from 56 percent in 2004.[123] A recent sample of policyholders through 2006 found take-up at about the same level, 58.3 percent.[124]

- Marsh also reports take-up as measured by the percentage of policyholders that purchase terrorism risk insurance coverage in a particular quarter. The take-up rate varies but generally shows an upward trend.

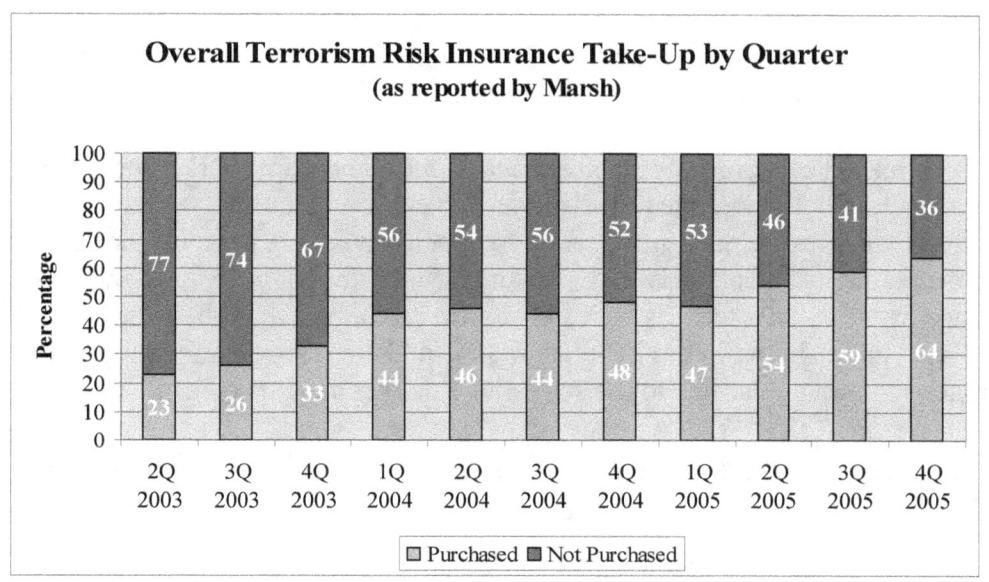

Source: Marsh

- Marsh found that take-up increased for each of 15 major industry groups. Financial institutions, real estate firms, and health care facilities have highest take-up at over 75 percent.[125]

- Specialty (standalone) and excess & surplus lines writers reported to Moody's take-up of only 10 to 35 percent.[126] Yet Aon reports that the general take up rate for standalone terrorism continues to rise.[127]

---

to 56.6 percent in 2006; a fixed sample of 189 of the same policyholders showed an increase in take-up from 49.5 percent in 2005 to 53.2 percent – confirming a continuing upward trend.

[123] Aon Corporation, "Property Terrorism Update – TRIA in the Balance," October 2005.

[124] Information provided by Aon Corporation. The sample included 480 Aon accounts with median TIV of $875 million, evaluated between August 1, 2005 through July 31, 2006.

[125] Marsh, Inc., Research Report, "Marketwatch: Terrorism Insurance 2006."

[126] Moody's Investors Service, Special Comment, "Terrorism Risk Remains Material for Insurers as TRIA Expiration Looms," June 2005.

[127] Aon Limitied, Aon Crisis Management, "Standalone Terrorism Insurance Market Update," March 2006.

- Marsh reports that all regions in the country have experienced increases in take-up rates, but there still is substantial regional variation from a high of 67 percent in the Northeast to 50 percent in the South. There is also substantial variation across states and cities.[128]

The increase in policyholder take-up would not be possible without insurers allocating additional capacity to terrorism risk insurance. New capacity enters the terrorism risk market by insurers that are providing coverage increasing the amount of terrorism risk that they provide and by new companies entering the market. The 2005 Treasury study found that 73 percent of insurers wrote some terrorism risk insurance coverage in 2002 (not including workers' compensation insurance), 91 percent in 2003 and 2004 and in early 2005, more than 97 percent of surveyed insurers reported writing polices with coverage for terrorism risk insurance in 70 percent of their policies.[129]

Increased capacity was also reported in the standalone market, both from existing and new entrants. Standalone terrorism market capacity continues to increase as measured by aggregate maximum per-risk capacity available from standalone market insurers and now stands at between $1.5 and $2 billion.[130] Both Marsh and Aon report new capacity from new terrorism risk insurance participants. Aon expects the existing standalone terrorism market to generate more standalone terrorism aggregate capacity and that new market entrants to the standalone market are expected.[131]

The Insurance Industry Appears Willing to Allocate Additional Surplus to Terrorism Risk

In summary, since the passage of TRIA: policyholder surplus levels have increased; insurer retentions of risk under TRIA have increased; prices for terrorism risk

---

[128] Marsh, Inc., Research Report, "Marketwatch: Terrorism Insurance 2006"; Robert Blumber, Marsh & McLennan Cos., "TRIA and Terrorism Insurance," PARMA Session presentation, February 10, 2006.

[129] U.S. Department of Treasury, Report to Congress, "Assessment: The Terrorism Risk Insurance Act of 2002," (June 30, 2005), pp. 3, 57, 59.

[130] Marsh estimates stand alone market property capacity as between $930 million to $2.03 billion. Marsh, Inc., Research Report, "Marketwatch: Terrorism Insurance 2006" (Marsh's figures include $25 million from ACE Limited which withdrew from the market in 2005); Marsh, Inc., Comments to the PWG dated April 20, 2006 (estimating between $1 billion and $2 billion). This amount is greater than the $1.37+ billion estimated by Marsh the year prior. Marsh, Inc., Research Report, "Marketwatch: Terrorism Insurance 2005." Aon estimates the standalone market's property capacity at $1.52 billion in 2006 (property), and $110 million to $170 million for casualty risks. Aon Corporation, Comments to the PWG dated April 21, 2006. Aon's estimate in the fourth quarter of 2005 standalone market capacity was at about $1.3 billion, continuing a growth trend since 2002. Aon Limited, Aon Crisis Management, "Standalone Terrorism Insurance Market Update," March 2006. This is up from its prior estimate of $1.270 billion for 2005 (property) and $1.210 billion in the second quarter of 2004 (property). Aon Corporation, "Property Terrorism Update – TRIA in the Balance," October 2005; Aon Corporation, "Property Terrorism Update," April 2005. This all compares with approximately $600 million in 2002. Guy Carpenter Seminar Report, Terrorism, The Terror Risk: Can It Be Managed?" Chapter 5: "Managing the Risk: The Marsh Perspective on the Terrorism Market," March 2002.

[131] Aon Corporation, "Property Terrorism Update – TRIA in the Balance," October 2005; Marsh Inc., Research Report, "Marketwatch: Terrorism Insurance 2006."

insurance have fallen or stabilized; and policyholder take-up rates have increased. The chart below summarizes the broad trends described in previous sections.

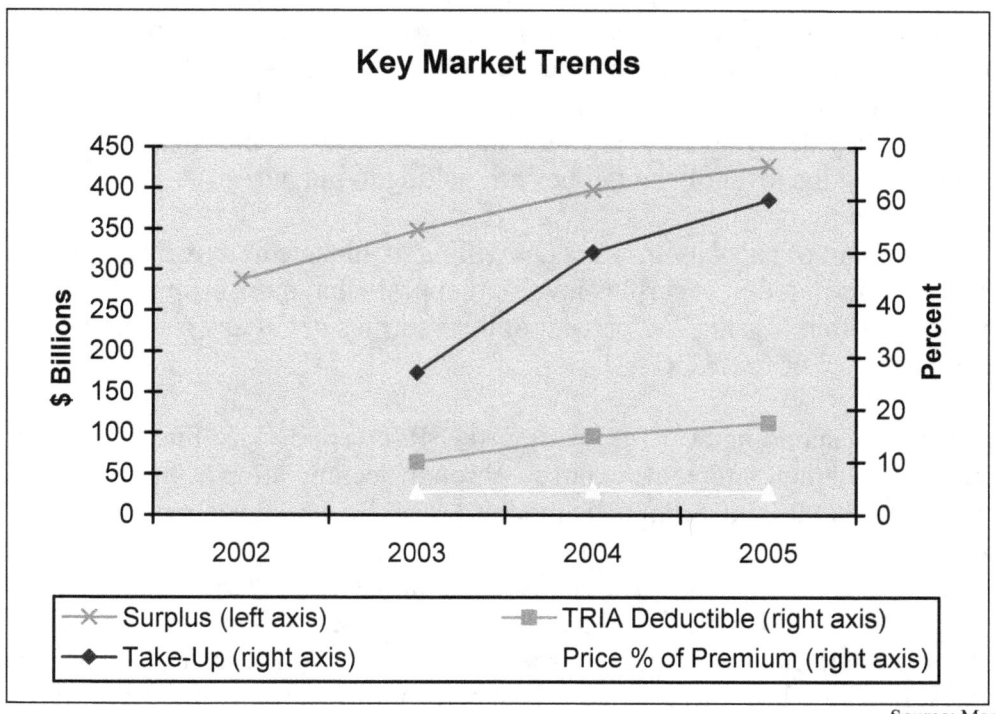

Source: Marsh/NAIC

A key trend in the chart above is that as the Federal government's role in the terrorism risk insurance market contracts, private market capacity has thus far provided adequate supply to respond to increased demand. In this regard, there appears to be some correlation between increased policyholder surplus levels and an increased supply of terrorism risk insurance as measured by the increased take-up rates. This general trend has occurred despite increasing risk retentions under the TRIA Program, and it has been accompanied by falling or relatively stable prices. The insurance market appears to have financially recovered from the September 11 attacks. It is certainly reasonable to expect the availability of terrorism risk insurance to increase as the property and casualty insurers' financial strength improves over time.

As overall policyholder surplus is not specifically allocated to particular lines of coverage, it is not generally a good indicator of the industry's maximum terrorism loss claims-paying ability, especially for lines of insurance covered under the TRIA Program. An insurance company's policyholder surplus serves a number of functions: paying expected claims for other policies in force for all lines of insurance (between commercial and personal lines) and cushioning variances in reserves.[132] Some insurance market observers have estimated that the amount of policyholder surplus available to pay terrorism claims for lines of insurance covered under the TRIA program is roughly 30

---

[132] See generally, David Cummins, "Should the Government Provide Insurance for Catastrophes?" Federal Reserve Bank of St. Louis *REVIEW* (July/August 2006).

percent of the surplus.[133] Recognizing this as well, Aon reported that it estimated the property and casualty industry's policyholder surplus level at $414 billion in the third quarter of 2005, but available capacity was likely closer to $171 billion in lines of insurance covered by TRIA (or 41 percent).[134] A recent report by the Insurance Information Institute estimates 2005 policyholder surplus at $427 billion with $169 billion available to cover terrorism risk.[135] Nonetheless, overall policyholder surplus appears to be a key determinant in insurers' allocation of available capacity to terrorism risk insurance and the level of capital they are willing to put at risk.

The amount of capacity insurers are willing to allocate to terrorism risk insurance does appear somewhat tied to surplus levels. It appears that most insurers try to retain their exposure within less than 10 percent of their surplus net of any reinsurance recovery (private reinsurance or from TRIA).

Insurers responding to A.M. Best's 2004 SRQ were divided into two groups: those that assessed their aggregate exposure through accumulation assessment (wide-area), and those that used deterministic models (A.M. Best assigned more confidence in these responses).[136] (See section B.1 for discussion of modeling approaches). Insurers that used accumulation assessment were asked to model their 5 largest concentrations of clustered buildings in 11 high-risk cities and outside those cities and to report on their largest loss. For attacks within the high-risk cities, 69 percent of insurers reported that their largest potential loss was at or below 10 percent of their policyholder surplus, net of any private reinsurance or TRIA recovery. Outside of the cities, 63 percent reported that their largest potential loss was at or below 10 percent of surplus. Insurers who used deterministic modeling were asked to model their 5 largest potential losses from a 5-ton to 6-ton truck bomb. Within the high-risk cities, 68 percent of insurers had a maximum potential loss at or below 10 percent of their policyholder surplus; outside of the cities, the corresponding percent of insurers decreased to 58 percent.

The data above suggest that insurers manage their exposure net of any Federal backstop recovery, and that overall available capital is an important determinant of the availability of terrorism risk insurance. This is also suggested by the fact that a majority

---

[133] See, Robert Hartwig, Gordon Stewart & Claire Wilkerson, "Terrorism, Insurance and the United States Government," Insurance Information Institute, September 2004 (based on analysis of 2003 policyholder surplus level). See also, Robert Hartwig, "The Fate of TRIA: Is Terrorism an Insurance Risk," Insurance Information Institute, presentation to National Insurance Association, June 2004, estimating that 40 percent of industry policyholder surplus backs property, liability, and workers' compensation lines (based on analysis of 2002 policyholder surplus levels).

[134] Aon Corporation, Comments to the PWG dated April 21, 2006, citing A.M. Best, "Special Report: U.S. P/C Industry Reports First Underwriting Profit Since 1978," April 25, 2005. See also, Center on Federal Financial Institutions (CoFFI), "TRIA Renewal: Policy Forum Proceedings," May 2005 (statements by AIA and ACE (citing Insurance Information Institute) estimating commercial lines surplus at approximately $175 billion in 2005).

[135] L. James Valverde, Jr. & Robert Hartwig, "9/11 and Insurance: The Five Year Anniversary," Insurance Information Institute, September 2006.

[136] A.M. Best, Special Report, "Terrorism: Too Risky Without TRIA?," December 2005 (The range of insurers is based on whether insurers measured exposure based on accumulation assessment or deterministic modeling).

insurers indicated that they would continue to provide some level of terrorism risk insurance following the expiration of the TRIA Program – and most at current capacity levels.

The Treasury study provided some evidence that some insurers were continuing to provide terrorism risk insurance extending into the first few months of 2006, despite the then-anticipated expiration of the TRIA Program at the end of 2005. The 2005 Treasury study found that roughly half of surveyed insurers, when asked about the policies written in January and February of 2005, reported that they would continue to provide terrorism coverage in 2006 comparable to that with TRIA in place. Of the half that would not provide comparable coverage post-TRIA, 77 percent reported they would exclude foreign terrorism and 24 percent would not exclude foreign terrorism but the coverage provided would not be comparable to what was provided with TRIA in-place (*e.g.*, policy sublimits, *etc.*).[137] Some responses may not reflect voluntary decisions as several states have refused to allow terrorism exclusions in the absence of a Federal backstop. In other words, approximately 62 percent of insurers planned to continue to offer terrorism insurance in some form. Of those that reported that they would continue to offer the coverage as they had with TRIA in place, insurers reported there would be no increase in cost.[138] Although this survey covered only policies issued in early 2005 extending into the first two months of 2006, it is generally consistent with some industry predictions of the post-TRIA market.

While it is reasonable to expect that some insurers will be unwilling to provide any coverage post-TRIA[139], insurers that continue to offer terrorism coverage will likely manage their aggregate terrorism retentions to a level similar to their deductible exposure under TRIA.[140] As Aon explained to the PWG:

> [M]ost insurers elected to severely limit their balance sheet exposure to TRIA. … It is not surprising that the vast majority of insurance carriers that were willing to continue to offer terrorism coverage beyond 2005 can be characterized as "large" … . This was due to the fact that TRIA recoveries were remote for these large, multi-line carriers due to their Direct Earned Premium writings. As such, these carriers simply continued to offer terrorism coverage up to an aggregate amount commensurate with their TRIA Deductible exposure in 2005. Given the small limits and high pricing associated with terrorism treaty reinsurance, the pricing and availability of private treaty reinsurance was of little consequence to a majority of carriers' "post TRIA" underwriting appetites.[141]

---

[137] U.S. Department of Treasury, Report to Congress, "Assessment: The Terrorism Risk Insurance Act of 2002," (June 30, 2005), pp. 75-76.

[138] U.S. Department of Treasury, *Ibid.*, p. 76.

[139] Marsh, Inc., Research Report, "Marketwatch: Terrorism Insurance 2006."

[140] Aon Corporation, "Property Terrorism Update," April 2005.

[141] Aon Corporation, Comments to the PWG dated April 21, 2006.

Market participants often stressed the limited appetite that insurers and reinsurers have for terrorism risk as well as potential availability and pricing challenges certain markets face. As Marsh explained in its comments to the PWG, in the absence of TRIA some areas will likely experience limited supply and higher prices:

> As we worked on property renewals for our clients at the end of 2005 in the midst of uncertainty as to whether or not TRIA would be extended, we learned a great deal about the potential long term availability and affordability of terrorism insurance in the absence of the federal backstop. The available capacity and the pricing varied tremendously depending on clients' exposures. For smaller business and large clients with little to no exposure in central business districts or without what are often referred to as "trophy or target" properties, we were pleasantly surprised by the markets' willingness to provide terrorism coverage beyond the expiration of TRIA. Pricing was reasonable and capacity was generally available.
>
> However, for clients with exposures in urban areas with a high concentration of risk, clients in high hazard industries (utilities or chemical manufacturers) or with properties viewed as "target" risks such as stadiums, or for our largest clients seeking maximum capacity, the situation was the opposite. Capacity was limited and the cost was very high.[142]

Conclusion

Since September 11, the insurance industry has recovered and there have been improvements in the financial health of insurance industry, which plays a role in how much capacity insurers are willing to expose to terrorism risk. Surpluses in the property and casualty industry have risen since September 11, as the industry has posted profits (even with the 2005 hurricane season losses), and has benefited from increased rates of return on assets. As a result, insurers appear to have more available capital to allocate, and they apparently have chosen to allocate additional capacity to terrorism risk as demonstrated by the increased sales since the inception of TRIA. The general trend observed in the market for terrorism risk insurance has been that as insurer retentions have increased under TRIA, prices for terrorism risk have fallen and take-up (purchase) rates have increased. Based on these observations, it appears that insurers should be willing to allocate additional capacity to terrorism risk over time, although it is difficult to speculate on the amount of capacity insurers are willing to devote to terrorism risk.

---

[142] Marsh, Inc., Comments to the PWG dated April 20, 2006.

B.5. State Regulation

Terrorism Risk Insurance and State Insurance Laws and Regulations

State laws and regulations govern various aspects of the insurance marketplace, including the approval of rates and forms, the imposition of financial solvency standards, and in some cases, the mandatory provision of certain types of coverage. The provision of terrorism risk insurance in commercial lines of insurance as required by TRIA falls within this general state regulatory structure.

One aspect of state regulation that has received a considerable amount of attention is "price controls" or, more precisely, the regulation of insurance rates used by insurers licensed or admitted in a state (referred to as the "licensed or admitted market"). The licensed or admitted market provides the bulk of commercial property and casualty insurance in the U.S., focusing mostly on standard insurance policies. While states do exert oversight over pricing, they generally do not formulate rates for their licensed insurers and require them to use those rates. Instead, insurers determine the rates they want to use in a particular state in which they are licensed, and then comply with the applicable rate regulation required in that state.

In general, insurers must be able to justify their rates, either by the use of their own loss data and projections, or by the utilization of rating information and loss cost factors developed by a national insurance advisory organization – such as the Insurance Services Office, Ltd. (ISO), the American Association of Insurance Services (AAIS), or the National Council on Compensation Insurance (NCCI). There are differing approaches to state price controls or rate regulation, including prior approval (rates must be filed and approved before they can be used), file and use (rates must be filed before they are used), use and file (rates can be used without pre-filing, but must be subsequently filed), flex rating (automatic approval of rate changes within a specified band), or information only (rates are filed for informational purposes only). For property and casualty insurance (excluding workers' compensation insurance, which is discussed later) 5 states have no rate filing requirements (*i.e.*, no rate regulation), 15 states require that rates are filed before they are used (*i.e.*, in general the most restrictive form of rate regulation), with the other states falling somewhere in between.[143]

While the state restrictions on pricing have received the most attention in regard to potentially limiting the ability of insurers to provide terrorism risk insurance coverage, other direct aspects of state regulation, such as form approval (just discussed above) and mandatory coverage requirements (most prominently in workers' compensation and fire coverage), or indirect aspects of state regulation, such as requiring rate re-filing and

---

[143] Five states have no filing requirements and are said to have a deregulated open market for commercial lines (No File); 1 state requires informational rate filings only (Information Only); 2 states provide for the automatic approval of rate changes within a specified band (Flex Rating); 9 states allow rates to the used without pre-filing, but they must be subsequently filed (Use & File); 15 states (plus D.C.) require rates to be filed before they are used (File & Use); and 18 states require rates to be filed and approved before they can be used, and generally allow rates to be "deemed" approved 30 days after they are filed, if the state has not taken any action during that time (Prior Approval with Express Deemer).

approval of sublimits, have also been cited as potential problems.[144] While there may be some potential regulatory burden associated with these other aspects of state insurance regulation, it is difficult to fully evaluate any separate impact they might be having on the market for terrorism risk insurance.

Exceptions to State Insurance Rate Regulation

In terms of pricing, although states regulate commercial insurance rates to various degrees, it is likely that a significant portion of commercial terrorism risk insurance for large commercial risks is exempt from state price regulation. These exemptions are either directly in place depending on the various measures of the size of the policyholder, or are indirectly permitted by allowing access to the surplus lines market.

The general principle behind the exemptions based on policyholder size is that large commercial buyers have the economic clout and insurance buying expertise to negotiate with insurers in a largely unregulated environment. The National Association of Insurance Commissioners (NAIC) has compiled a chart outlining the various state criteria for exemption of large property and casualty commercial lines (see Appendix). There is considerable variation in how states implement these large policyholder exemptions. For example, in the District of Columbia, a commercial property and casualty policy with an aggregate insurance premium of over $10,000 is exempt, while in Georgia, premium must be in excess of $50,000 ($250,000 for risks with multi-state locations) before exemptions are permitted, and the insured must also have 25 or more full-time employees, assets of over $1.5 million, and annual revenues of $2.5 million or more. Due to these differences, it is difficult to estimate how much of the total commercial property casualty insurance business is written directly under these various state exemptions.

In addition to large policyholders having direct access to the unregulated insurance market, businesses that cannot obtain coverage in the licensed or admitted market can access what is known as the surplus lines market.[145] Most states require that a business attempt to obtain coverage in the licensed or admitted market, and if those attempts are not successful it can obtain coverage in the surplus lines market. The surplus lines market is not subject to state rate or form regulation.

While it is difficult to determine exactly how many policyholders access the surplus lines market and why they are using the surplus lines market, A.M. Best found in

---

[144] In terms of mandated coverage for terrorism risk insurance, almost all states mandate coverage for terrorism risk (and war risk) for workers' compensation insurance. In addition, some states require that property insurers cover losses from fire resulting from a terrorist attack through the adoption of the the New York Standard Fire Policy (SFP). Twenty-eight states have SFP laws that apply to a broad set of insurers, 12 allow fire caused by a terrorist act to be excluded, leaving 16 states requiring coverage for fire following a terrorist act.

[145] The surplus lines industry provides a market for insurance for risks that are hard to place and generally not insured by the licensed or admitted market. Generally referred to as the "surplus lines market," these insurers are not licensed to do businesses in a state but are allowed to issue insurance if placed by a state-licensed surplus lines broker.

a 2006 Special Report that in 2005 there were $33.3 billion in surplus lines premiums written on a nationwide basis, which accounted for 12.65 percent of total commercial lines insurance premiums.[146] This is a slight increase from $33 billion in surplus lines premiums written in 2004, although the overall market share was higher at 14.14 percent.[147] The nationwide percentage of surplus lines premiums may understate the importance of the surplus lines market in large states or urban areas. For example, in New York, after September 11 and before the enactment of TRIA, more commercial policyholders purchased terrorism risk insurance from the surplus lines market than had before, and by early 2004, they had not returned to the licensed or admitted market where rates and forms are subject to state regulation. Excess line premium writings from the surplus lines market had tripled in New York from 2001 to 2003, from about $685 million in 2001 to over $2 billion in 2003.[148] Excess line premiums have continued to increase, from $2.6 billion in 2004 to $2.8 billion in 2005.[149]

Many Insurers Are Not Charging for Terrorism Risk Insurance

While state price controls can lead to various inefficiencies in the insurance marketplace (described more fully in relation to workers' compensation below), restrictions in place in the licensed or admitted market may not be having a large impact in some portions of the market.

The 2005 Treasury study found that while the trend was for more insurers to charge for terrorism risk insurance, a significant percentage of insurers were still not charging for insurance coverage. In 2002, over 75 percent of insurers stated that they provided coverage for terrorism risk in their property policies at no charge, with the percentage of insurers not charging for coverage falling to 46 percent in 2003 and 40 percent in 2004. Limited 2005 data suggest that 35 percent of insurers still charged nothing for terrorism risk insurance coverage.[150] Similarly, 70 percent of policyholders said they received terrorism risk insurance coverage for free in 2002, falling to 42 percent in 2003, and just over 37 percent in 2004.[151]

In addition, Treasury estimated that approximately 57 percent of policyholders had non-certified terrorism risk insurance coverage in 2004 and 2005 and that the majority received the coverage for free.[152] Moody's found that among both national and regional carriers, small company take-up is between 90 and 100 percent, driven by the

---

[146] A.M. Best, Special Report, "Surplus Lines Market 2006," September 2006.

[147] A.M. Best, Special Report, "Excess and Surplus 2005," September 2005.

[148] Gregory Serio (Superintendent of Insurance), Statement of New York State Insurance Department before U.S. House of Representatives Subcommittee on Capital Markets, Insurance, and Government Sponsored Enterprises and the Subcommittee on Oversight and Investigations, April 28, 2004.

[149] Information from the Excess Line Association of New York as supplied by the New York State Insurance Department. Figures are surplus lines premium assigned to risks located in New York and not gross premiums reported in the State.

[150] U.S. Department of Treasury, Report to Congress, "Assessment: The Terrorism Risk Insurance Act of 2002," (June 30, 2005), pp. 4, 63.

[151] U.S. Department of Treasury, *Ibid.*, pp. 88-89.

[152] U.S. Department of Treasury, Report to Congress, "Assessment: The Terrorism Risk Insurance Act of 2002," (June 30, 2005), p. 88.

fact that the coverage is typically provided at a nominal fee or in many instances for free.[153]

To the extent states have exerted any control over rates for commercial property and casualty insurance they have approved positive, but small charges in some instances. The extent to which insurers are not charging for terrorism risk insurance coverage for a portion of their policyholders does not seem to be a direct reflection of state rate controls. It appears likely that some segment of the market will continue to receive free coverage long term, as they did prior to September 11. The 2005 Treasury study results suggest that these are likely to be smaller insureds in markets with little perceived terrorism exposure where insurers cannot justify positive terrorism risk insurance prices to their customers.[154]

Workers' Compensation Insurance

Workers' compensation insurance is generally considered to be a separate line of insurance from other commercial property and casualty coverages. It is more highly regulated and subject to a greater amount of price regulation and coverage mandates, including terrorism insurance. Unlike other types of commercial property and casualty insurance, workers' compensation insurance generally does not have large policyholder exemptions or a surplus lines market that operates outside of the state rate controlled environment. Instead, many states have either established their own state-run monopolistic workers' compensation programs (North Dakota, Washington, Ohio, and West Virginia) or have established a residual market structure to provide coverage for policyholders that cannot obtain coverage directly from insurance companies.

Economists have long pointed to price controls as leading to inefficient outcomes. If the mandated price is set above the market clearing price, the result will be surpluses; if the mandated price is set below the market clearing price, the result will be shortages. Shortages are generally observed in insurance markets with strict price controls. Residual markets, known also as "shared" or "involuntary" markets or "markets of last resort," are state-sponsored mechanisms that provide businesses with the ability to obtain workers' compensation coverage. In general, if an insurer is not willing to undertake a particular workers' compensation risk at the state-approved rates, that business will be placed in the residual market. Any profits or losses from policies in the residual market are shared proportionally with all insurers that provide workers' compensation insurance in a particular state. As the size of the residual market increases in a particular state, insurers evaluate their willingness to continue providing workers' compensation insurance in that state; and, in general, this type of structure likely limits the number of insurance companies that are willing to provide coverage in a particular state.[155]

---

[153] Moody's Investors Service, Special Comment, "Terrorism Risk Remains Material for Insurers as TRIA Expiration Looms," June 2005.

[154] Based on consultations with the National Association of Mutual Insurance Companies (NAMIC), which explained that with small, regional mutual insurers, the inability to price the coverage and perception of low exposure were the key drivers in the coverage being provided at no charge.

[155] See generally, Scott Harrington & Patricia Danzon, "Rate Regulation, Safety Incentives, and Loss Growth in Workers Compensation Insurance," *Journal of Business*, Vol. 73, No. 4 (2000); Patricia Danzon

Despite the long-standing structural problems with the workers' compensation market, insurers have generally remained in the market, even as their TRIA retentions have increased, and despite their inability to fully price for terrorism risk.[156] According to the National Council on Compensation Insurance (NCCI), as illustrated in the table below, the number of companies writing workers' compensation in each of the non-monopolistic states (excluding those companies that reported zero premium or are in runoff and not writing new business) has remained relatively stable since the passage of TRIA.

Number of Workers' Compensation Insurers by State[157]

STATE	2002	2003	2004	2005	Percentage Change 02-05
AK	141	136	128	126	-10.64%
AL	225	222	222	225	0.00%
AR	223	215	215	222	-0.45%
AZ	204	208	205	211	3.43%
CA	230	210	213	217	-5.65%
CO	212	201	202	206	-2.83%
CT	208	197	193	203	-2.40%
DC	190	187	184	190	0.00%
DE	210	192	195	202	-3.81%
FL	223	228	230	247	10.76%
GA	291	282	283	286	-1.72%
HI	141	133	133	132	-6.38%
IA	259	242	234	238	-8.11%
ID	176	162	157	160	-9.09%
IL	299	280	285	287	-4.01%
IN	281	274	283	280	-0.36%
KS	236	221	221	221	-6.36%
KY	239	227	231	234	-2.09%
LA	194	187	196	201	3.61%
MA	214	194	195	200	-6.54%
MD	255	249	239	245	-3.92%
ME	142	131	136	139	-2.11%
MI	253	240	238	240	-5.14%

& Scott Harrington, "Workers' Compensation Rate Regulation: How Price Controls Increase Costs," *Journal of Law and Economics*, Vol. XLIV (April 2001); Anthony Barkume & John Ruser, "Deregulating Property-Casualty Insurance Pricing: The Case of Workers' Compensation," *Journal of Law and Economics*, Vol. XLIV (April 2001).

[156] Decisions by insurers to remain in the workers' compensation market may also be impacted by "exit barriers" that are imposed in some states. For example, a state may require that if an insurers stops writing workers' compensation insurance, it must stop writing all lines of insurance within the state; or, a state may require financial contributions to the workers' compensation residual market mechanism; or, a state may only permit a gradual withdrawal over time.

[157] Five states are not included in the table because they are monopolistic in that workers' compensation insurance is available only through a state-created insurance mechanism; the five are: North Dakota, Ohio, Washington, West Virginia, and Wyoming. (West Virginia is in transition to a private system).

STATE	2002	2003	2004	2005	Percentage Change 02-05
MN	242	227	226	229	-5.37%
MO	249	236	237	244	-2.01%
MS	225	212	222	226	0.44%
MT	168	160	157	158	-5.95%
NC	251	245	248	253	0.80%
NE	224	220	220	218	-2.68%
NH	194	178	183	190	-2.06%
NJ	263	241	238	246	-6.46%
NM	190	186	187	190	0.00%
NV	172	175	174	173	0.58%
NY	279	253	240	247	-11.47%
OK	218	211	212	222	1.83%
OR	197	189	190	188	-4.57%
PA	301	282	277	283	-5.98%
RI	175	153	158	160	-8.57%
SC	243	242	242	242	-0.41%
SD	200	190	189	194	-3.00%
TN	281	270	270	272	-3.20%
TX	266	250	247	254	-4.51%
UT	185	179	182	180	-2.70%
VA	266	260	255	263	-1.13%
VT	172	158	158	163	-5.23%
WI	272	257	260	261	-4.04%

Source: NCCI

Some states have seen larger declines (*e.g.*, 11 percent in New York state or 32 companies), but for 30 out of 46 states (including D.C.) the decline in number of companies has been less than 5 percent, or there has been slight increase. The table above does not indicate a particularly vibrant workers' compensation market in terms of increased competition from new entrants, but given the structural problems of the workers' compensation market it is not clear that increased risk exposure for terrorism risk insurance under TRIA has had any broad negative impact.

Fire Insurance

Some states require that property insurers cover losses from fire from all causes (except war), based on the 1943 New York Standard Fire Policy (SFP). Twenty-eight states have SFP laws, however, since September 11, 12 of the 28 SFP states now allow fire caused by terrorism to be excluded. (A table of states is included in the Appendix). Sixteen states still mandate coverage for fire caused by terrorism (in some of these states the requirement may not apply to surplus lines insurers or to exempted policies, as discussed above). State-mandated fire coverage interferes with insurers' capacity allocation decisions and this effect may lead to inefficient distribution of capacity making terrorism risk insurance less available overall. However, given that SFP has not been adopted by 22 states and 12 states have modified the SFP to allow terrorism exclusions, any impact on capacity allocation is difficult to evaluate.

54

Conclusion

While state laws and regulations have the potential to significantly interfere with the operation of insurance markets, it does not appear that such restrictions have had a significant impact in the market for terrorism risk insurance to date. In the long term, state actions related to broader mandates for coverage of terrorism risk or rate restrictions could impact the ability of insurers to manage and underwrite terrorism risk.

B.6. Buyer Behavior

Despite Falling or Stable Prices for Terrorism Risk Insurance, Many Policyholders Are Not Purchasing Coverage

The general trends noted in section B.4 illustrate that since the passage of TRIA, pricing for terrorism risk insurance has declined or remained relatively stable in the 3 to 5 percent range of overall insurance costs.[158] At the same time, policyholder take-up rates have generally increased from 30 to 60 percent, which implies that about 40 percent of policyholders are not purchasing terrorism risk insurance despite favorable market conditions.[159]

The general trends on policyholder take-up of terrorism risk insurance were described in section B.4. Some representative examples on a nationwide basis include the following:

- The 2005 Treasury study found that take-up rates among policyholders increased from 27 percent in 2002 to 39.5 percent in 2003, and to 54 percent in 2005. The 2005 results imply that about 46 percent of policyholders still choose not to purchase terrorism risk insurance.[160]

- More recently, Aon reported that for the 12 months ending on April 1, 2006, 40 percent of accounts did not obtain any terrorism risk insurance coverage.[161]

---

[158] The general trends on pricing for terrorism risk insurance illustrated in section B.4 reflect an average cost for terrorism risk insurance measured as a percentage of a policyholder's overall insurance costs. On a more disaggregate basis, Marsh documented different terrorism risk percentage costs by industry, ranging from as high as 5 to 9.5 percent for financial institutions, roughly 5 to 6 percent for the real estate industry, to as low as 2 to 3 percent for others. Marsh, Inc., Research Report, "Marketwatch: Terrorism Insurance 2006."

[159] The policyholder "take-up" information presented in this section refers to the ratio of commercial policyholders that elect to purchase terrorism insurance, contrasted by those that decline the coverage. It does not include those policyholders that are provided terrorism coverage as part of their policies at no additional charge, as the coverage is generally accepted in such instances. It also does not include buyers of workers' compensation insurance or other state-mandated terrorism coverage.

[160] U.S. Department of Treasury, Report to Congress, "Assessment: The Terrorism Risk Insurance Act of 2002," (June 30, 2005), pp. 3, 84.

[161] Aon Corporation, "2006 Property Report, A Tale of Two Markets" 2006. For the year prior, the Wharton Risk Center examined 478 Aon accounts over the 12 months ending May 2005 and found 42

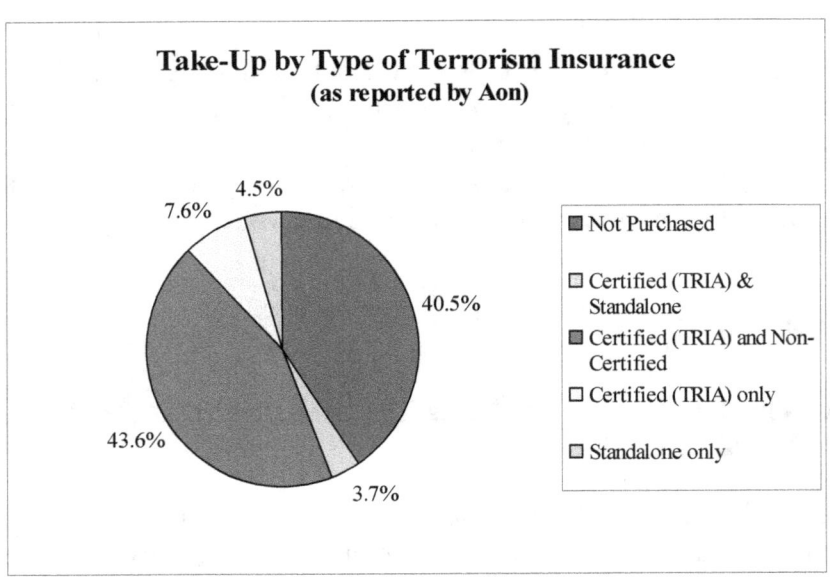

Take-Up by Type of Terrorism Insurance
(as reported by Aon)

4.5%

7.6%

40.5%

43.6%

3.7%

- Not Purchased
- Certified (TRIA) & Standalone
- Certified (TRIA) and Non-Certified
- Certified (TRIA) only
- Standalone only

Source: Aon

Similar trends showing increasing take-up rates with still a relatively high proportion of policyholders not purchasing terrorism risk insurance have also been found in surveys at the regional level. Examples include the following:

- Marsh reported the following city take-up rates for 2004: Boston – 69 percent; Washington, D.C. – 60 percent; Chicago – 58 percent; Dallas – 57 percent; New York City – 54 percent; Philadelphia – 49 percent; Detroit – 42 percent; Los Angeles – 39 percent; San Francisco – 37 percent; and Houston – 23 percent.[162]

- Marsh found that on a broader regional basis in the South and West take-up remains just at 50 percent. In the Midwest and Northeast, take-up now exceeds 50 percent, yet still some 30 to 40 percent of policyholders forego terrorism risk insurance.[163]

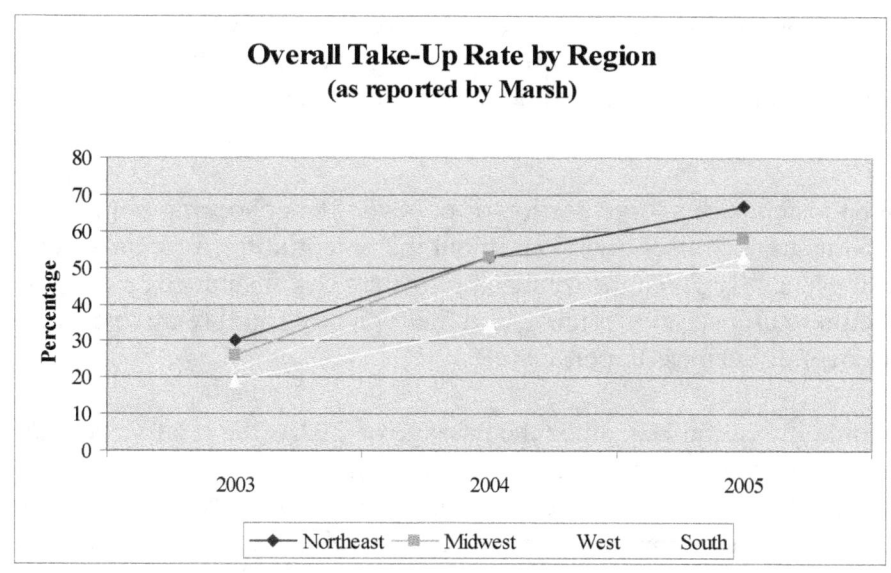

Source: Marsh

- Marsh also reports that 2005 take-up rates vary considerably by State: New York (65 percent); Illinois (59 percent); New Jersey (55 percent); Texas (50 percent); California (50 percent); and Florida (36 percent).[164]

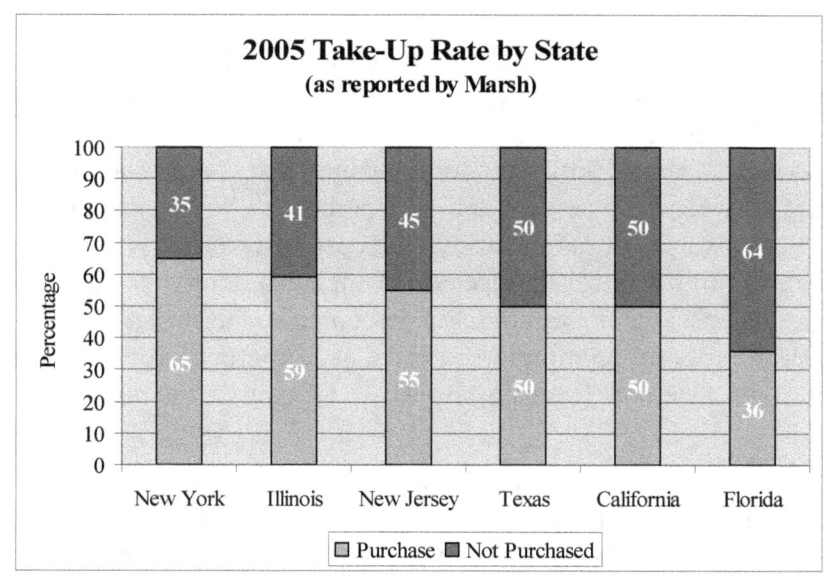

Source: Marsh

---

[163] Marsh Inc., Research Report, "Marketwatch: Terrorism Insurance 2006."

[164] Robert Blumber, Marsh & McLennan Cos., "TRIA and Terrorism Insurance," PARMA Session presentation, February 10, 2006

The data presented above indicate that while policyholder take-up for terrorism risk insurance has increased, there still appears to be a lack of willingness on the part of a large number of policyholders to purchase any terrorism risk insurance. In addition, there is wide variation across regions with some major cities and states (*e.g.*, Houston, San Francisco, and Florida) having in excess of 60 percent of policyholders not purchasing terrorism risk insurance in 2004 or 2005. Even in New York City, the data above show approximately 46 percent of policyholders not purchasing terrorism risk insurance in 2004.

The persistence of a large portion of policyholders choosing not to purchase terrorism risk insurance raises questions about the potential for future market development, especially given the trends in terrorism risk insurance pricing, overall trends in commercial insurance pricing, and the typically small relative cost of insurance compared to overall business expenses.

As noted in section B.4, since the passage of TRIA, the relative cost of terrorism risk insurance compared to overall insurance costs has generally declined or remained relatively stable. In addition, the insurance market has generally moved into a relatively soft phase of overall declining prices.[165] Such a combination would typically result in an overall lower dollar cost for terrorism risk insurance. From 2005 to 2006, Marsh found across a broad range of accounts (generally larger policyholders that Marsh serves), that differ from year-to-year, the median premium for terrorism insurance increased from $12,500 to $13,145. A smaller sample of same accounts over that same time period found the median premium of those accounts fell significantly, from $37,700 to $16,750.[166]

Finally, overall insurance costs in many industries appear to be relatively small when compared to overall business expenses. In terms of some specific industries, in the wholesale and retail trade and selected service industries, the share of insurance costs (exclusive of workers' compensation) to total business expenses is approximately 1.65 percent (ranging between 0.55 percent and 4.31 percent).[167] For most businesses (although these costs vary across industries), the cost of terrorism risk insurance coverage is a small percentage of overall insurance cost, which is a relatively small percentage of overall business expenses. For example, the percentage of terrorism risk insurance premium to overall property premium is reported at 2.5 percent (retail), 2.9 percent (food and beverage), and 5.1 percent (transportation).[168] Of course, the numbers represent

---

[165] See generally, Council of Insurance Agents & Brokers, "Prices Up, Capacity Down for Cat Exposures; Other Commercial Markets Soften, The Council Survey Shows," News Release and Survey, July 19, 2006, reporting quarterly survey results of declining commercial rates; Standard and Poor's, "U.S. Commercial Lines Midyear 2006 Outlook: Sector Enjoying Exceptional Earnings," RatingsDirect, June 2005; A.M. Best, Statistical Study, "U.S. Property/Casualty Industry Reports Underwriting Profit in First Half of 2006, September 18, 2006.
[166] Marsh, Inc., "Terrorism 2006 – Year to Date," presentation to PWG staff, July 2006.
[167] Economics and Statistics Administration, U.S. Department of Commerce Department, Business Expenses and Cost of Insurance from 2002 Economic Census, Industry Series.
[168] Marsh, Inc., Research Report, "Marketwatch: Terrorism Insurance 2006."

industry-wide aggregate data, and there will be substantial variation in the actual costs to individual policyholders in each industry, and across other industries.

Buyer Perception of Risk Appears To Be an Important Factor in the Policyholder Purchase Decision

The demand for terrorism coverage, or policyholder willingness to purchase coverage, is an important factor in the overall development of the market for terrorism risk insurance. A.M. Best recently surveyed insurers and reported that low policyholder interest is among the barriers to private insurers offering terrorism risk insurance.[169] Many businesses appear to believe that if a terrorist attack occurs it will not happen to them. A lack of information on terrorism risk, no new attacks on U.S. soil, cost of insurance, and the expectation of government disaster aid are likely contributing to purchase decisions. As illustrated above, a fair portion of businesses are forgoing terrorism insurance – even at relatively low premiums.[170] While price is an important determinant in purchase decisions, buyers' perceptions of terrorism exposure play an equally important role.[171]

A number of surveys have been conducted since September 11 regarding policyholders' perception of risk. Some examples include the following:

- In early 2002 prior to the enactment of TRIA, Marsh reported that of 150 commercial accounts seeking quotes for terrorism coverage from the standalone market (a key source of coverage at the time), all received offers of coverage. Fifteen percent purchased coverage while 15 percent declined to purchase, and the remaining 70 percent were undecided. Reasons cited for not purchasing coverage were potential Federal action and the perception that pricing was expensive for coverage that in the past had been provided for free or at minimal cost. Marsh also reported that when Congress adjourned in January 2002 without passing TRIA, demand and purchases increased.[172]

- Shortly after TRIA was enacted, The Council of Insurance Agents & Brokers (CIAB)[173] conducted a survey of its members. Half of the brokers responding said that fewer than 20 percent of their clients were buying terrorism insurance. Reasons cited included high cost and the belief among policyholders that they

---

[169] "Saying No," *Best's Review*, (September 2006).

[170] Howard Kunreuther, Erwann Michel-Kerjan & Beverly Porter, "Assessing, Managing and Financing Extreme Events: Dealing with Terrorism," National Bureau of Economic Research, November 20, 2003; Howard Kunreuther & Mark Pauley, "What You Don't Know Can Hurt You: Terrorism Losses and All Perils Insurance," The Wharton School, University of Pennsylvania, December 2004.

[171] Swiss Re, Comments to the PWG dated April 20, 2006.

[172] Guy Carpenter, Seminar Report, "Terrorism, The Terror Risk: Can It Be Managed?" Chapter 5, "Managing the Risk: The Marsh Perspective on the Terrorism Market," March 2002.

[173] The Council of Insurance Agents & Brokers is an association of insurance brokers who collectively handle about 80 percent (as measured by premium) of the nation's commercial property and casualty insurance.

were not at risk.[174] In a follow-up survey reported 4 months later, 72 percent of the brokers indicated that their commercial customers were still not purchasing terrorism insurance coverage. Ninety percent said that customers turned down terrorism coverage because they thought they did not need it; others thought it was too expensive.[175]

- In the fall of 2003, Kaye Insurance Associates, a New York-based insurance brokerage, reported that only 36 percent of New York area companies indicated that they had purchased terrorism insurance (54 percent of the real estate industry). Among those without terrorism insurance, the reasons it was not purchased were because the clients said they were not a target (66 percent), or that coverage was too costly (17 percent), or too limited (13 percent).[176]

- In 2004, the American Association of Insurance Services (AAIS) conducted a survey of terrorism insurance practices. Of 42 property and casualty companies responding, 16 reported that half of their clients purchased terrorism coverage; 12 reported some purchases (but less than half of their clients); and 11 reported very few clients were purchasing the coverage. Of the 42 respondents, 36 reported that of those not purchasing the coverage, the principal reason was that policyholders viewed their exposure to loss from a terrorist act to be remote.[177]

- In 2004, the Risk and Management Society (RIMS) conducted a survey of 133 risk managers. Of those, 85 responded to a question as to the reasons why they did not purchase terrorism insurance: 32 (37.6 percent) explained that it was "Price – decision that the risk was not enough to warrant expense"; 30 respondents (35.3 percent) reported they did not purchase terrorism insurance because there was "No perceived need – operations not near areas perceived to be exposed to terrorist threat."[178]

- In July 2005, the Council of Insurance Agents & Brokers reported with its Commercial Property/Casualty Market Index that the total number of customers buying terrorism insurance remained "relatively small". The brokers responding

[174] "Many Commercial Interests Are Not Buying Terrorism Insurance, New CIAB Survey Shows," *PRNewswire* (March 24, 2003); Expert Commentary, "CIA Shows Businesses Rejecting Terrorism Coverage," www.irmi.com, March 2003.

[175] "A Glass Half Full: As The Terrorism Risk Insurance Act Approaches Its First Anniversary, Demand for Terrorism Insurance Is Low, But Industry Experts Say the Backstop Is Bringing Capacity and Stability to the Marketplace," *Best's Review* (September 1, 2003).

[176] "Brokers' Client Survey Finds Pricing and Solvency More a Concern than Terrorism," *Bestwire* (October 13, 2003); "Commercial Property Coverage Concerns New Your Insurance Brokers," *Bestwire* (December 17, 2003).

[177] Accessed at http://aaisonline.com/services/terrorsurvey.html.

[178] The National Alliance and Risk and Insurance Management Society (RIMS) May 2004 Terrorism Survey. The relatively low percentage of respondents who believed their organizations were not at risk is probably a reflection of the relatively large size and complexity of organizations that hire risk managers. Such organizations are relatively likely to include at least one location near geographical areas perceived to be exposed to terrorism.

to the survey indicated that the main reasons customers do not buy terrorism coverage are the belief that they are not likely targets and the cost of coverage.[179]

- The 2005 Treasury study's policyholder survey revealed that among those policyholders who did not buy terrorism risk insurance, there was a substantial increase from 2003 to 2004 in the number who felt they were not at risk: in 2004, 89 percent explained it was because they did not feel they were at risk, up from 49 percent in 2003. Also among non-purchasers there was an increase in the percentage not buying the coverage because of high cost, up from 24 percent in 2003 to 36 percent in 2004.[180]

For some purchasers of terrorism risk insurance, such as commercial real estate owners, the decision to purchase terrorism risk insurance can be influenced by the requirements of lenders and investors that some level of terrorism risk insurance coverage be purchased. Commercial lenders typically require commercial real estate borrowers to secure "all risk" property insurance, including terrorism risk insurance, covering the property securing the financing. Loan documents typically require terrorism risk insurance subject to its being commercially available and at a reasonable rate. Lenders often have the ability to force-place coverage if it is not obtained by the borrower. Improvements in lender monitoring of underlying insurance coverage of borrowers have likely contributed to increased take-up of terrorism risk insurance. For example, the real estate sector appears to have the largest take-up rate among industries: 79 percent in 2005, up from 60 percent in 2004 and 30.2 percent in 2003.[181] The increase in take-up from 2004 to 2005 also correlates with a dramatic rate decrease from 0.0117 percent of total insured value during 2004 to 0.0067 percent in 2005, indicating that pricing also was likely an important factor.[182]

Not included in the above data is information on workers' compensation insurance. The take-up rate for workers' compensation is generally 100 percent as most states, with the exception of Texas, require employers to purchase workers' compensation insurance and almost all states require such insurance to include coverage for workplace injuries and death occurring as a result of terrorism and war. Purchase is mandated by law without correlation to price, which (as discussed in section B.5) is heavily rate controlled.

---

[179] The Council of Insurance Agents & Brokers, "Commercial P/C Market Softens More In Second Quarter, Council Survey Shows," News Release, July 2005.

[180] U.S. Department of Treasury, Report to Congress, "Assessment: The Terrorism Risk Insurance Act of 2002," (June 30, 2005), p. 109. See fn. 177 for an explanation for the relatively high percentage of policyholders responding to the Treasury survey that believed they were not exposed to terrorism risk. By design, Treasury's survey included a large number of small organizations, which may view themselves as not being exposed to substantial risk. Note also that the Treasury policyholder sample size is more than 15 times that of the RIMS survey cited above.

[181] Marsh, Inc., Research Report, "Marketwatch: Terrorism Insurance 2006"; Marsh, Inc., Research Report, "Marketwatch: Property Terrorism Insurance 2004."

[182] Marsh, Inc., Research Report, "Marketwatch: Terrorism Insurance 2006."

Increased Demand is Important To Long-Term Availability

As with any market, in the market for terrorism risk insurance the demand side plays a key role. Purchasers of terrorism risk insurance evaluate prices for coverage along with their own perceptions of risk in making a decision whether to purchase coverage. As standard economic theory would predict, there does appear to be a correlation between higher take-up rates and the improvements in the pricing environment surrounding terrorism risk insurance in recent years. However, even with relatively low prices for terrorism risk insurance and take-up at its highest reported level since September 11,[183] many policyholders are not purchasing terrorism risk insurance. Going forward, buyers' perception of their risk exposure and their willingness to pay for terrorism risk insurance coverage will be key factors on the demand side of the market. Until policyholders alter their perception of risk and increase their willingness to pay for terrorism risk insurance coverage, further market development may be impeded. Expectations of post-disaster Federal assistance[184] may also factor into buyers' cost-benefit analyses, although there is little evidence of this in general terrorism risk markets.[185] As noted above, while insurers and reinsurers are determining how much capital to allocate to terrorism risk, some greater response would be expected if policyholders are willing to pay higher prices. Low market penetration in a voluntary market at low prices does not lead to the economic volume needed to attract new capital.[186] Long term, some additional capacity is likely to respond to demand at higher prices.

Conclusion

Long-term availability of terrorism risk insurance depends in large measure on demand. If demand increases and buyers are willing to pay premiums commensurate with the risk they seek to transfer, then over time capacity should rise to meet demand. Given that a significant number of policyholders are not purchasing coverage for terrorism risk insurance, even as prices have declined in recent years, there will most

---

[183] Aon Corporation, "Property Terrorism Update – TRIA in the Balance," October 2005.

[184] Prior to September 11, Federal disaster aid to commercial entities was typically limited to federally-subsidized loan programs, such as those administered by the U.S. Small Business Administration. Federal aid to compensate for commercial losses resulting from the September 11 attacks expanded to include direct compensation systems, such as grants, and tax benefits to affected businesses. See generally, Lloyd Dixon & Rachel Kaganoff Stern, "Compensation for Losses from the 9/11 Attacks," RAND Institute for Civil Justice (2004).

[185] As some economists have noted, the Federal government cannot commit to not providing such disaster relief to uninsureds. Wharton Risk Management and Decision Processes Center, "TRIA and Beyond," The Wharton School, University of Pennsylvania, August 2005. See also, Lloyd Dixon, *et al.*, Occasional Paper, "Issues and Options for Government Intervention in the Market for Terrorism Insurance," RAND Center for Terrorism Risk Management Policy, 2004, p. 10; Howard Kunreuther & Erwann Michel-Kerjan, "Dealing with Extreme Events: New Challenges for Terrorism Risk Coverage in the U.S.," Wharton Risk Management and Decision Processes Center, April 2004, p. 20; Robert Rhee, "Terrorism Risk in a Post-9/11 Economy: The Convergence of Capital Markets, Insurance, and Government Action," *Arizona State Law Journal.*, Vol. 37, No.2 (2005) .

[186] Swiss Re, Comments submitted to PWG dated April 20, 2006.

likely be an impact on the amount of capacity that insurers are willing to allocate to terrorism risk.

C. Group Life Coverage

This section focuses on the long-term availability and affordability of terrorism risk insurance for group life insurance, which was a specific part of the PWG's mandate. Many of the factors that impact the overall market for terrorism risk insurance (discussed in section B) are generally applicable with regard to group life insurance. Rather than repeat that background information in this section, this report analyzes many of the same factors in the context of the market for group life insurance.

Group life insurance, as its name suggests, is underwritten on a group basis. Insurers treat the group as a single risk rather than underwriting the mortality risk of each of the group's individual members. The group usually consists of employees of a company or members of an association, labor union, credit union, or other organization (as permitted under state law).[187] The employer or sponsoring organization is the policyholder and is issued a master policy under which the insurer agrees to insure the lives of the participating members of the policyholder's group. The individual employees or group members are the insured persons and are referred to as "certificate holders," as they are issued certificates of insurance evidencing their coverage under the master policy. The premium is often paid by the employer, or is shared between employer and employee. Additional premiums for supplemental coverage (above the base benefit the employer is willing to sponsor) are usually paid by the employee.

There are many different products that constitute group life insurance, such as renewable group term life insurance, group permanent insurance, group accidental death and dismemberment (AD&D) coverage, and group credit life insurance. The most common form of group life insurance is yearly renewable group term life insurance, which is the primary focus (unless otherwise noted) of the analysis that follows in this section. Face amounts of group term life insurance coverage are most commonly some multiple of earnings, a fixed or flat dollar amount, or based on a scale tied to earnings or position in the organization.[188]

---

[187] See generally, National Association of Insurance Commissioners Model Act: "Group Life Insurance Definition and Group Life Insurance Standard Provisions Model Act," NAIC Model Laws, Regulation and Guidelines (2006).

[188] In 2005, 53 percent of workers with group life insurance had benefits based on a "fixed multiple of earnings" formula; 36 percent of employees had benefits based on a "flat dollar amount", and others had either variable multiples or dollar amounts. U.S. Department of Labor's National Compensation Surveys of Employee Benefits in Private Industry in the United States, March 2005.

C.1. Group Life Market Conditions

Group Life Insurance and the Terrorism Risk Insurance Act

September 11 resulted in the loss of approximately 3,000 lives. Financial compensation mechanisms for the loss of life included charities, the September 11 Victims Compensation Fund and other Federal programs, workers' compensation insurance (*i.e.,* death benefits), and individual and group life insurance. Moody's reported that September 11 resulted in approximately $1-$2 billion in both individual and group life insurance payments. This represented about 4 percent of the $40 billion in annual death benefits paid by life insurers in an average year, and losses were modest on an individual company level.[189] Group life insurance losses from September 11 are often estimated at about half of the total $1-$2 billion in life insurance losses. Aon presented the PWG with an estimate of between $600 million to $800 million (including AD&D).[190] As compared with the property-casualty insurance industry's aggregate loss, September 11 was not as significant an insured loss event for the U.S. life industry.[191]

Group life insurance has never been part of the TRIA Program. When TRIA was enacted it did not include participation by group life insurance providers. Instead, Treasury was required to evaluate market conditions and determine whether to include group life insurance in the TRIA Program if both insurance and reinsurance were not available, or not likely to be available in the future.[192] In August 2003, Treasury found no appreciable reduction in the availability of group life insurance coverage for consumers, although it did find a general lack of catastrophic reinsurance.[193] Therefore, Treasury determined that group life insurance was not to be added to the TRIA Program. In December 2005, when TRIA was extended for two years, although there was some debate on the inclusion of group life insurance, it was again not included as part of the TRIA Program.

Group Life Insurance Remains Widely Available

For most U.S. employers (especially large to medium size), employer-provided group life insurance has become a standard employee benefit. Employer-sponsored group life insurance is usually provided as part of an overall package of employee benefit

---

[189] Moody's Investors Service, Special Comment, "Moody's Looks at Terrorism Risk in the U.S. Life Insurance Industry," February 2006.

[190] Aon Corporation, Comments to the PWG dated April 21, 2006, citing the American Academy of Actuaries. As a comparative reference, group life insurers collectively paid out approximately $19 billion in group life death benefits in both 2003 and 2004. Life Insurers Fact Book 2005, American Council of Life Insurers.

[191] As one study noted, "The impact of a catastrophe that kills hundreds or even thousands of people, tragic though it may be in human terms, may be only a marginal event in terms of the additional financial costs to the insurance industry." Risk Management Solutions, Inc., "Catastrophe, Injury, and Insurance," 2004, p. 4.

[192] TRIA Section 103(h)(1).

[193] U.S. Department of Treasury, Office of Public Information, "Treasury Announces Decision on Group Life Coverage Under Terrorism Risk Insurance Program," August 15, 2003.

products and premiums, which, although priced and purchased separately, are sometimes discounted based on the volume of the overall benefits purchased.

By all accounts, competition in the employee benefits market – including the market for group life insurance – is very robust. Group life insurers have long argued that due to the competitive nature of the market, they have little ability to raise prices or limit coverage and attempts to manage risk exposure in this manner would result in the loss of business to other providers. Competitive pricing, which has always occurred for large accounts, has also recently been observed with small to midsize accounts.[194] Overall, group life insurers concede that competitive pressures have made coverage available, even in the absence of TRIA protection or adequate private catastrophic reinsurance.

Broad trends of group life insurance certificate-holder take-up verify continued availability.[195] Some key empirical results include the following:

- Group life insurance certificates in-force totaled 165 million in 2004 (up from 162.6 million in 2003), with a total face amount of $7.63 trillion – a $1.1 trillion increase from the year before.[196]

- Fifty-two percent of workers in private industry had access to life insurance provided through their employer in 2005. This increased from 51 percent in 2004 and 50 percent in 2003[197] – the same period as the original three years of the TRIA Program. Similar trends were observed on a regional basis.

- Fifty-two percent of workers within metropolitan areas had access to life insurance provided through their employer in 2005, compared to 51 percent in 2004 and 50 percent in 2003; whereas 51 percent had access in non-metropolitan areas (a slight decline from 52 percent in 2004 but up from 49 percent in 2003).[198]

- In 2005, nearly 94 percent of employees who had access to employer-provided life insurance obtained some coverage and employee contributions toward life insurance typically were not required (89 percent of workers that participated did not have to contribute premiums).[199] The lack of a required employee contribution for group life insurance likely explains high take-up among employees.

---

[194] A.M. Best, Statistical Study, "Group Life Market Competition Persisted in 2004," August 29, 2005.
[195] As stated earlier, this report analyzes the group life insurance market overall. There are likely instances where particular groups face limited offers of coverage or higher prices. However, clear evidence of such instances is difficult to determine.
[196] Life Insurers Fact Book 2005, American Council of Life Insurers.
[197] U.S. Department of Labor's National Compensation Surveys of Employee Benefits in Private Industry in the United States (March 2005; March 2004).
[198] U.S. Department of Labor's National Compensation Surveys of Employee Benefits in Private Industry in the United States (March 2005; March 2004) and 2002-2003 (January 2005).
[199] U.S. Department of Labor, *Ibid.*, (March 2005).

Pricing for Group Life Insurance has Generally Decreased in Recent Years

In addition to group life insurance remaining widely available despite not having access to the TRIA Program, prices have also generally decreased since September 11. Unlike some segments of the property and casualty industry (most prominently workers' compensation insurance), states do not regulate rates charged by group life insurers.[200] It is unclear to what extent state regulators require that terrorism be covered by not allowing the use of terrorism exclusions in group life insurance policies (assuming insurers wanted to use them), or prohibit insurers from limiting their maximum single-event loss through the use of per-event loss limits. Nonetheless, the competitive aspects of the group life insurance market have continued to push prices down in recent years. Some examples of this trend include the following:

- Swiss Re in its comments to the PWG reports that group life rates have decreased since September 11 and are currently between 7 and 12 percent below their previous levels.[201]

- According to Gen Re Life Health's 2005 U.S. Group Life Market Survey (of 33 participating companies representing $16.7 billion in premium), premium rates for new sales decreased 8 percent from the year before.[202]

- A LIMRA International (LIMRA) survey (of 34 group life companies representing 85 percent of the total group life market) found that the overall cost per thousand dollars of new group life coverage remained relatively unchanged between 2004 and 2005 at $2.67 per thousand of coverage.[203]

As noted above, robust competition in the group life market appears to be driving decreases in pricing. One group life insurance representative explained the decision insurers face in this highly competitive group life insurance market as follows:

> To grow business in this highly competitive market, an insurer must take business away from a competitor. A decision to stop writing business in a given location would be difficult to make up elsewhere. In addition, re-entering the market in the area once exited would require the insurer to "buy back" accounts through discounted premium rates. In addition, because group life insurance is sold as part of a package of benefits, if group life insurance is not offered it may have an impact on the sale of other products.[204]

---

[200] National Association of Insurance Commissioners, Comments to PWG dated April 21, 2006.
[201] Swiss Re, Comments to the PWG dated April 20, 2006.
[202] Gen Re, Life Health, "2005 U.S. Group Life Market Survey, Executive Summary," 2006.
[203] LIMRA International, "Annual Review," Group Life Insurance Annual Review, 2005.
[204] Group Life Coalition, Comments to the PWG dated April 21, 2006.

Further, in geographic areas where insurers continue to do business, group life insurers explain that it is difficult (or they are unable) to price terrorism risk, and the highly competitive market environment prevents them from arbitrarily raising rates.[205]

Conclusion

Overall, among the comments received by the PWG, along with further consultations regarding group life insurance, there was general agreement – including group life insurer trade groups – that in the current market, group life insurance is generally available and affordable. For example, ACLI stated in written comments to the PWG: "currently, terrorism risk has had no measurable market impact on the availability and affordability of group life insurance coverage to policy and certificate holders."[206]

Despite not being eligible to participate in the TRIA Program, group life insurance still appears to be widely available in the private market and there has not been any impact on cost to policyholders. In the long term, given the likelihood of the continuing competitive nature and structure of the group life insurance market, there appears to be no reason to believe that current market conditions will not persist.

C.2. Reinsurance

Group Life Reinsurance

Group life insurers generally purchase two types of reinsurance: excess of loss on individual lives (covering high value insured lives individually), and catastrophic coverage (sometimes called per occurrence excess of loss) on its entire portfolio of policies. September 11 is reported to have had little impact on the availability and cost of excess of loss on individual lives reinsurance, but did impact the market for catastrophic reinsurance.

Prior to September 11, catastrophic life reinsurance was relatively inexpensive. Catastrophic life reinsurance premiums were historically low based on the market's general perception of the low probability of a catastrophic event affecting life insurers. Following September 11, much like the reinsurance market for property and casualty insurance, reinsurers initially withdrew from the group life market.

Capacity for catastrophic life reinsurance has gradually returned to the market. Overall, the ACLI reported that total group life insurance premiums ceded to reinsurers in 2004 were $3.9 billion, up from $3.675 billion in 2003.[207] Swiss Re noted that there has been a general trend of increasing demand for life reinsurance and prices have risen when compared with pre-September 11 pricing. Swiss Re did note, however, that the cost of terrorism risk catastrophe reinsurance gets less expensive with each year that passes

[205] American Council of Life Insurers, Comments to the PWG dated April 21, 2006.
[206] American Council of Life Insurer, *Ibid.*
[207] Life Insurers Fact Book 2005, American Council of Life Insurers.

without a terrorist attack in the U.S.[208] The general trend of increased availability of catastrophic life reinsurance – with higher prices, modified reinsurance treaty terms, and certain limits (*i.e.*, deductibles and policy limits) – has been noted by a number of market observers.[209] It is reasonable to expect that reinsurance would be available, but at different levels, higher prices, and on different terms than prior to September 11 (when reinsurance was apparently abundant and less expensive). These current market conditions reflect the same general return of capacity to the market as seen in the property and casualty market.

In addition to traditional reinsurance, there is a private industry catastrophe risk pool, the Special Pooled Risk Administrators, Inc (SPRA) available for group life risks. As of June 30, 2006, the Group Pool provided approximately $334 million in reinsurance coverage per company, up to an aggregate payout of $835 million per single event.[210] In comments to the PWG, Aon reported that additional pools had been established focusing on specific geographic areas, such as by small Midwestern carriers, as well as the establishment of the Shared Adverse Fluctuation Experience (SAFE) Pool providing catastrophic reinsurance for companies with low concentration in major metropolitan areas.[211]

The availability and cost of catastrophic life reinsurance leave group life insurers with choices. Group life insurers can purchase whatever reinsurance is available at higher costs and then attempt to adjust pricing to policyholders to reflect this increased cost. This option is available to group life insurers because, as noted above, unlike some segments of the property and casualty industry (most prominently workers' compensation insurance), states do not regulate rates for group life insurance. Alternatively, group life insurers can forgo purchasing the more expensive reinsurance and retain the risk themselves. The ACLI explained during consultations that although available, the majority of group life insurers have minimal, if any, catastrophic reinsurance. As the group life industry is a very competitive market, group life insurers appear unwilling to pass on their increased reinsurance costs or the implicit cost of higher risk retentions to their policyholders.

Conclusion

Since September 11, just as with property and casualty reinsurance (see section B.3), some catastrophic life reinsurance has returned and is available in the marketplace, *albeit* at higher cost when compared to pre-September 11 pricing. Today, group life insurers are deciding either to purchase reinsurance or to retain most of the risk – a

---

[208] Swiss Re, Comments to the PWG dated April 20, 2006.

[209] Aon Corporation, Comments to the PWG dated April 21, 2006; A.M. Best Company, *Review/Preview, Life Health Edition*, (January 2006); Moody's Investors Service, Special Comment, "Moody's Looks at Terrorism Risk in the U.S. Life Insurance Industry," February 2006; National Association of Insurance Commissioners, Comments to the PWG dated April 21, 2006; Swiss Re, Comments to the PWG dated April 20, 2006.

[210] Information provided by Swiss Re, which administrates the SPRA. The pool has a total net amount of risk of approximately $1.7 trillion.

[211] Aon Corporation, Comments to the PWG dated April 21, 2006.

decision that has not had any impact on the availability and affordability of group life insurance to consumers. It is reasonable to expect catastrophic reinsurance to become more available if group life insurers are willing to purchase such coverage. Nevertheless, the fact that many group life insurers are electing not to purchase catastrophic reinsurance suggests that they are have made a decision to retain their terrorism exposure.

C.3. Measuring and Managing Risk Accumulations

Aggregation Risk and Group Life Insurance

Group life insurance presents aggregation risk exposure to group life insurers in that a large number of employees covered under a single group policy or across multiple group policies may be concentrated in an office building, city block, or other geographic area. In contrast, individual life insurance policies are likely to be distributed more widely among different insurers. This type of group life aggregation risk stems from any geographically-centered mass-casualty event, whether terrorism or earthquake, or where insureds are concentrated, for example, from employee risk of infection from pandemic or biological attack. Aggregation risk is inherent in the nature of group insurance, much like workers' compensation insurance, and will continue long term. Much like property and casualty insurers, group life insurers have ways to measure and manage this aggregation exposure.

As discussed in section B.1, one way insurers manage aggregation risk is by not insuring too many policyholders (certificate holders for group life insurers) in the same geographic area, dense metropolitan block, or office building. Prior to September 11, life insurers in general did not monitor their aggregation exposure. As noted in section B.1, property and casualty insurers have made great strides in managing their aggregation exposures. It remains unclear what steps group life insurers have taken to better manage aggregation risks.

Management of Aggregation Risk by Group Life Insurers

In 2006, Moody's reported the results of a terrorism risk survey of U.S. life insurers, including group life writers (representing some of the largest individual and group life writers, and collectively 75 percent of the market based on 2004 premiums) and found that overall, life insurers (both individual and group life writers) lag behind property and casualty insurers in their ability to quantify and model their potential terrorism exposures. The key reasons Moody's reported for the lack of responsiveness of the life insurers were: the relatively low level of September 11 life insurance losses; the geographic dispersion of certain types of life insurance business; inadequate policy-level data; and the high cost of modeling versus its perceived value. Moody's concluded that over time the gap may narrow; but for now, "life insurers are considerably behind."

Indeed, 40 percent of those surveyed, both group and individual life providers, indicated they had not changed their business practices following September 11.[212]

Some 70 percent of surveyed life insurers assessed accumulations by geographically mapping their larger risk exposures, although data quality varied (policyholder versus certificate holder location). Beyond mapping locations of their risks, however, only approximately 33 percent actually quantified their maximum loss exposure in some way (such as through aggregation or deterministic models). However, as compared to individual life companies, Moody's noted that group insurance providers appear to have the most advanced mapping and modeling capabilities but that notable exceptions exist. Although an earlier report of Moody's found that most life insurers have sufficient geographic diversification in their portfolios to mitigate terrorism risk,[213] it concluded that most companies could benefit from better and more complete mapping (*i.e.*, certificate holder level) and modeling of their business. With few exceptions, most respondents to its survey had no plans to expand or develop their current terrorism risk assessment approaches.

As explained in section B.1, modeling aggregate exposure is dependent on the quality and quantity of policy-level data. It appears that improvement in this area can be made by group life insurers. As Aon and consultations revealed, often group life insurers know the billing address or main headquarters of their policyholder, the employer, but not the location of each individual certificate holder.[214] As this is a matter of better data collection, improvement could be made in this area, and such improvements could help group life insurers to better manage their aggregation exposures.

It is not clear to what extent group life insurers can also manage their aggregation risk by use of terrorism exclusions or sublimits. Group life insurers initially reported to the PWG that state insurance regulators did not allow them to use terrorism exclusions as part of their group life insurance policies.[215] This claim was, to some degree, inconsistent with information provided by the NAIC and various state regulators. The NAIC pointed out that unlike workers' compensation insurance, there are no statutory prohibitions on the use of exclusions in group life insurance policies.[216] Others that were consulted also made this point.[217] Further, group life policy forms are reportedly not subject to regulatory approval in all states, and in those states where approval is required, the NAIC believes that group life insurers have not sought approval of terrorism exclusions for two reasons: first, as NAIC acknowledges, regulators would likely not approve exclusions; and second, competitive pressures cause group life insurers to decide against seeking approval of terrorism exclusions. The American Council of Life Insurers (ACLI)

---

[212] Moody's Investors Service, Special Comment "Moody's Looks at Terrorism Risk in the U.S. Life Insurance Industry," February 2006.
[213] Moody's Investors Service, Special Comment, "Terrorism Risk Remains Material for Insurers as TRIA Expiration Looms," June 2005.
[214] Aon Corporation, Comments to the PWG dated April 21, 2006.
[215] Comments received from, and consultations with the American Council of Life Insurers and the Group Life Coalition.
[216] National Association of Insurance Commissioners, Comments to the PWG dated April 21, 2006.
[217] Aon Corporation, Comments to the PWG dated April 21, 2006.

explained that, despite early assertions, it could not definitively state that terrorism exclusions did not exist in any group life policies, nor could it report how many states do not allow exclusions.[218] In fact, the District of Columbia permits terrorism exclusions, while other states, such as New York, do not.[219] The ACLI, in clarifying its earlier assertion, pointed out that Kansas and North Carolina allow the use of terrorism exclusions under some circumstances.[220] In the light of the above, it is reasonable to conclude that, as the NAIC suggests, the extent to which group life insurers may not be using terrorism exclusions seems to be more the result of competitive, rather than regulatory pressure.

Although terrorism exclusions apparently are not being be used by some insurers, one way insurers may be able to manage aggregation risk is by lowering limits on group policies,[221] such as per-certificate coverage maximums[222] or by using per-event aggregate policy limits (*i.e.*, limit of liability provision).[223] Some group life insurance policies establish the maximum amount the insurer will pay for losses from a single event, regardless of the number of lives lost or the aggregate exposure of the certificate-holders' face amounts of coverage. In this way, group life insurers can manage the maximum probable loss from a single plan and manage aggregation exposure. However, it is not clear to what extent aggregate policy limits are used or how willing some group life insurers are to employ these tools.

It is also worth noting that most group life insurers manage their overall company exposure by writing other types, or lines, of insurance. Most group life insurers are multi-line writers and are able to diversify among lines and books of business. According to the Insurance Information Institute, of the 30 largest group life insurers, only 2 had 90 percent or more of their net written premiums in that line in 2004; 1 had 36 percent; another, 27 percent; and the rest had 20 percent or less of their business in group life insurance.[224]

Conclusion

Group life insurers are capable of managing their aggregate exposures much in the same way as property and casualty insurers, but it is unclear to what extent group life insurers have made use of these tools. Further improvements by group life insurers in

---

[218] American Council of Life Insurers, letter to PWG staff dated September 8, 2006.

[219] Based on consultation with the National Association of Insurance Commissioners.

[220] The American Council of Life Insurers explains that terrorism exclusions may be approved in these states only if an insurer can unequivocally demonstrate to regulators that without the use of such exclusions, the insurer will become insolvent. Such a standard appears designed to address the often-heard claims by some group life insurers that they may become insolvent in the event of certain terrorist attacks, due to their inability to exclude terrorism from their policies.

[221] Moody's Investors Service, Special Comment, "Moody's Looks at Terrorism Risk in the U.S. Life Insurance Industry," February 2006.

[222] Aon Corporation, Comments to PWG dated April 21, 2006.

[223] National Association of Insurance Commissioners, Comments to PWG dated April 21, 2006.

[224] Insurance Information Institute, "Pandemic: Can the Life Insurance Industry Survive the Avian Flu?," January 2006.

managing aggregation risk would be expected to have a positive impact on the ability of group life insurers to manage aggregation exposure.

D. Chemical, Nuclear, Biological and Radiological Coverage

This section focuses on coverage for chemical, nuclear, biological and radiological (CNBR)[225] events. Coverage for CNBR, when used in the context of terrorism, usually refers to insurance for losses resulting from or arising out of chemical dispersal attacks, nuclear weapon detonations, bombings of nuclear facilities, infectious biological attacks, and radiological dirty bombs. CNBR coverage for terrorism risk is often considered separately from general terrorism risk coverage given the nature and potential magnitude of such losses, and the historic treatment of such losses in the insurance industry.

D.1. Market Conditions

Factors that Impact Overall Availability and Affordability of Terrorism Insurance for CNBR Losses

Historically, insurance coverage for losses associated with CNBR has had more to do with the nature of CNBR losses themselves rather than the particular cause of the loss. For the most part, insurers did not cover CNBR losses even before September 11, and do not cover CNBR losses associated with terrorism today even with a Federal backstop in place. As the NAIC noted, "since the policy forms either include or exclude coverage for CNBR events without distinction as to the cause of the event, there should be no difference in the availability of coverage for such events caused by acts of terrorism."[226]

One of the key factors affecting reinsurer and insurer unwillingness to insure CNBR events is the potential size and magnitude of the losses. As discussed in sections B.2 and B.3, modeling organizations have made great progress in quantifying the expected insured losses that might result from various terrorist attacks. Severity of loss depends on the type of attack, location of the target, and assumptions (such as weather conditions, *etc.*). In terms of a CNBR attack, questions remain as to whether such models can provide reasonable estimates of losses given all the variables, or whether they can even quantify certain types of losses, such as liability. Unlike conventional terrorism, insurers have had almost no experience with large-scale CNBR attacks or their resultant losses (*i.e.*, no loss experience upon which to estimate future losses). In addition, some losses from CNBR events would be long-tail in nature, which adds to the difficulty of estimating potential losses. Despite problems associated with modeling CNBR events, some scenarios that were submitted to the PWG had losses ranging anywhere from $2

---

[225] There are other acronyms, such as NBC, NBCR, CBRN, and WMD. We have used the acronym based on the word order used by Congress in TRIEA.

[226] National Association of Insurance Commissioners, Comments to the PWG dated April 21, 2006.

billion to $158 billion in property losses, and from $22 billion to $484 billion in workers' compensation losses.[227]

While insurers have made great strides in managing accumulation risk associated with conventional terrorist attacks, the task involving CNBR risks is more difficult given the potential geographic scale of some modeled events. The potential for widespread damage and losses makes it difficult to limit losses by managing aggregation exposures. In addition, potential losses may be of such magnitude and so widespread, both geographically and by multiple lines of business, that there is less potential risk spreading. In addition, potential losses are of such magnitude that insurers would have even greater difficulty in developing actuarial prices.

Even if insurers were willing to underwrite CNBR terrorism risks, it would be difficult for insurers to transfer or spread such risks onto reinsurers or the capital markets. In contrast to the reinsurance market for conventional terrorist attacks, coverage for CNBR losses is typically excluded from most reinsurance contracts. There is, however, some limited reinsurance capacity for CNBR exposure. According to the RAA and others, CNBR capacity is in the range of $900 million to $1.6 billion, which is approximately 15 to 20 percent of the estimated $6 billion to $8 billion in terrorism reinsurance capacity for conventional terrorist acts (see section B.3). To the extent the risk is retained, a large-scale CNBR event could lead to losses that would exceed an insurer's surplus and capital. In addition, the likely disruptive effects a large-scale CNBR event might have on the overall economy and capital markets would likely affect insurers' asset returns and hamper their ability to secure additional capital in order to meet claims.

Background on Coverage for CNBR Losses

As discussed in section I.A, most commercial property insurance coverage is written on what is called an "all risk" or "all perils" insurance policy, which covers loss to the insured property from all causes except those that are expressly excluded. Apart from whether a policy has a terrorism exclusion or not, there are other exclusions that apply to CNBR events. Generally, with workers' compensation insurance, CNBR losses – no matter how caused – cannot be excluded. In addition, as described below, states that have adopted the Standard Fire Policy require that fire resulting from a CNBR event be covered no matter how the fire was caused. So in these cases, either all or a portion of the losses associated with a CNBR terrorism event may be covered. Whether such losses are covered or excluded depends on the particular circumstances surrounding the loss and the terms of the insurance policy.

Also, as discussed in section I.A, TRIA requires that insurers make available coverage for acts of terrorism on the same terms and conditions as other types of coverage offered as part of the insurer's commercial property and casualty insurance policies. In making coverage available, insurers are not required to make coverage

---

[227] American Academy of Actuaries, Comments to the PWG dated April 21, 2006. Probabilities for the example loss severities were not provided.

available for losses from a CNBR terrorist act if coverage for CNBR exposure is not part of the overall policy regardless of the cause of the CNBR damage. Thus, insurers are not required to offer terrorism coverage from CNBR losses if such exclusion is also applied to losses arising from events other than acts of terrorism, and is permitted by state law.

Nuclear and Radiological Exclusion

Even prior to September 11, state insurance regulators had long approved exclusions in property polices for losses caused by nuclear reaction, nuclear radiation or radioactive contamination. Since September 11, both reinsurers and insurers have clarified their policy language regarding these exclusions.[228] For policies containing such exclusions, a nuclear attack would not likely be covered, depending on the particular exclusion. Although policy language may vary, some examples follow.

Examples of Nuclear Exclusions

ISO Special Form CP 1030	The insurer "will not pay for loss or damage caused directly or indirectly by … nuclear radiation, or radioactive contamination, however caused."
Absolute nuclear exclusion	Bars recovery from "any injury or damage to or arising out of any nuclear device, radioactive material, isotope … or any other chemical element having an atomic number above eighty-three (83) or any other material having similar properties of radioactivity."
NAIC Atomic Energy Exclusion Model Law. (Adopted in some form in 23 states)	Allows insurers to attach a written statement to policies notifying policyholders that the policy does not "cover loss or damage caused by nuclear reaction or nuclear radiation or radioactive contamination, all whether directly or indirectly resulting from an insured peril under said policy."
ISO's Nuclear, Biological or Chemical Terrorism Exclusion (Other Than Certified Acts of Terrorism); Cap on Losses from Certified Acts of Terrorism (developed post-TRIA)	Excludes losses from "the use, release or escape of nuclear materials," "radiation or radioactive contamination," as well as "the dispersal or application of pathogenic or poisonous biological or chemical materials."

Despite the general presence of nuclear exclusions, fire losses due to a nuclear attack would likely be covered in some states with Standard Fire Policy laws (see section B.5). Generally, in those states, fire from all causes (except war) is covered. Since a nuclear detonation results in fire, losses from fire that follows a nuclear reaction may be

---

[228] See generally, Swiss Re, "Nuclear Risks in Property Insurance and Limitations of Insurability" 2003; ISO Properties, Inc., for exclusions in various standard forms.

covered in certain Standard Fire Policy states (however radiological contamination without fire damage would generally not be covered). However, some states have allowed terrorism exclusions to be added to fire policies. Sixteen States do not allow terrorism exclusions. As such, coverage will depend on the terms of each policy and applicable state law.

Operators of nuclear power facilities are also required to have coverage for nuclear and radiological exposures. The Price-Anderson Act[229] provides liability limits and a multi-layered insurance mechanism covering third-party liability (and not first-party property damage) from certain nuclear incidents, which can include acts of terrorism. The Nuclear Regulatory Commission must determine whether an incident is substantial enough to trigger Price-Anderson. Under the Act, licensed nuclear reactor operators are required to first purchase the maximum amount of liability insurance available from private insurers. Operators do this by purchasing approximately $300 million in offsite liability coverage per reactor from an insurance pool – American Nuclear Insurers (ANI) – made up of private insurance companies. Above the $300 million in coverage, the operators themselves participate in an excess layer of coverage pool (administered by ANI), paid for through post-loss, pro-rata (per-reactor) assessments levied on each operator, which provides up to $95.8 million per reactor (in installments not to exceed $15 million per year); this pooled excess layer has a total current capacity of approximately $10 billion.[230] Once these indemnification sources are exhausted, the operator has no further liability and Congress must determine how third-party victims are to be compensated.[231]

Pollution Exclusion

Various forms of what is broadly referred to either as the "pollution exclusion" or the "absolute pollution exclusion" are prevalent in insurance policies. While most property and general liability policies contain some type of pollution exclusion, there is no standard language. A representative form excludes coverage "for loss or damage caused by or resulting from … discharge, seepage, migration, release or escape of pollutants" unless caused by certain events. Most policies define terms, such as "pollutant", broadly. Various courts interpret the exclusion differently depending on the language used, the particular circumstance involved, and jurisdictional precedents. In general, most insurers would expect that their adopted version of the pollution exclusion precludes coverage for biological and chemical losses associated with an act of terrorism.

CNBR Terrorism Exclusion

Prior to TRIA's passage, state insurance regulators in most states approved a terrorism exclusion for use by admitted carriers (as discussed earlier, surplus lines

---

[229] Pub. L. 85-256, 71 Stat. 576.
[230] Information provided by the U.S. Nuclear Regulatory Commission.
[231] The Price-Anderson Act is designed to provide third-party liability coverage for nuclear facility operators. In terms of insuring the facilities themselves, property coverage is provided by pools, such as Nuclear Energy Insurers Ltd., formed by U.S. operators of nuclear plants.

insurers are free from state form regulation and did not need such pre-approval). The exclusion most states approved for admitted carriers generally provided that terrorism resulting in total losses of less than $25 million or where no more than 50 people were injured (a relatively small-scale attack) could not be excluded – except in the case of CNBR. Terrorism involving CNBR could be excluded regardless of the size of the total loss or the number of persons hurt.[232] The state-approved exclusion permitted the following CNBR terrorism acts to be fully excluded from coverage if the terrorism was carried out by means of:

- The dispersal or application of radioactive material, or through the use of a nuclear weapon or device that involves or produces a nuclear reaction, nuclear radiation, or radioactive contamination; or
- Radioactive material is released, and it appears that one purpose of the terrorism was to release such material; or
- The terrorism is carried out by means of the dispersal or application of pathogenic or poisonous biological or chemical materials; or
- Pathogenic or poisonous biological or chemical materials are released, and it appears that one purpose of the terrorism was to release such materials.[233]

In consulting with the NAIC, it could not be determined why regulators had concluded that insurers could cover and would be responsible for $25 million in losses if incurred by a conventional terrorist attack, but not $25 million incurred as a result of a CNBR-terrorist attack, given that the loss level would be the same. Regulators explained that the broad exclusion for CNBR was approved due to the historical treatment excluding all losses associated with this risk.

Workers' Compensation Insurance

State law requires that workers' compensation policies cover CNBR events, whether or not caused by terrorism, thereby mandating (and ensuring) availability. Workers' compensation awards are established by state statute and regulation. Workers' compensation insurance, which virtually every state (except Texas) requires employers to purchase, covers the employers' liability for workers' compensation awards. The scope and amount of coverage provided in workers' compensation policies is set by statute, and all carriers in the state must use the same policy form. In mandating the terms, states have not allowed insurers to exclude coverage for awards due to injury or death caused by terrorism, or by CNBR events caused by terrorists or otherwise, or even for acts of war.[234] In addition, states exert a significant amount of control over workers' compensation insurance pricing, as noted in the section B.5.

---

[232] As discussed in Section A, some states, such as New York, did not approve any terrorism exclusions but still allowed exclusions for various types of CNBR losses, however caused.

[233] See generally, standard forms of ISO Properties, Inc.

[234] TRIA covers workers' compensation insurance for losses caused by certified acts of terrorism, as well as losses caused by war (exclusive line).

It appears that workers' compensation coverage for CNBR events, terrorist-caused or otherwise, will remain widely available and affordable as a matter of state public policy. State insurance regulators explained that they did not foresee any changes to this over the long term, and insurers agreed.[235] However, workers' compensation insurers do face certain challenges. As they have explained, before September 11, reinsurance for workers' compensation covered all events, including acts of terrorism and CNBR events. Since September 11, reinsurance has excluded CNBR events. Workers' compensation insurers cannot exclude terrorism or CNBR in their policies, and while they can control accumulation, it is not clear how effective that is given the potential scale of some types of CNBR events (*e.g.*, plume clouds). Workers' compensation insurers are also not as free to control overall exposure as are other property and casualty insurers. Although a workers' compensation carrier can decline to insure a potential policyholder, if an employer cannot acquire any insurance from any market participant voluntarily (called the "voluntary market"), it must obtain coverage from a residual market in which all workers' compensation insurers doing business in the state must participate and share in that risk. However, as noted in section B.5, despite increasing retentions under TRIA and the potential for large CNBR exposures, insurers have generally remained in the market.

Potential for Broad Increases in CNBR May be Limited

Other than where state law mandates that CNBR terrorism insurance be provided (such as with workers' compensation), there appears to be some limited amount of capacity currently available for special coverage for loss arising solely from contamination by chemical or biological substances, subject to various limitations, such as sublimits. Such coverage is available on a standalone basis from non-admitted surplus lines insurers. In addition, the maximum coverage limit available may be in the range of only $10 to $50 million (compared to an average of $200 million for conventional terrorism). The coverage is reported to be expensive as compared with other insurance (5 percent Rate on Line, or rate on loss limit). In addition, some policyholders are obtaining liability coverage by purchasing environmental or pollution liability policies that include terrorism coverage, but at low limits.

One consequence of TRIA, however, is that CNBR coverage can be obtained through use of captive insurers accessing the TRIA Program. A captive insurer is an insurance company that insures the risk of its owner and is managed by the owner with or without the help of a captive management company. In effect, this is a more formal method of self-insurance and lacks the risk transfer that traditional insurance provides. Captives are insurers for purposes of the TRIA program, and with their relatively low TRIA deductibles, have quicker access to the Federal backstop than a traditional insurer. As a result, captives have been promoted as a means of obtaining CNBR coverage at relatively little expense and some coverage in the market may exist as a result. However, in the long term, captives are unlikely to provide capacity for CNBR coverage without access to a Federal reinsurance backstop.

---

[235] Consultations with the National Association of Insurance Commissioners and insurer groups.

Given the historical lack of coverage for CNBR in the absence of a specific mandate, the responses to the PWG's request for comments cast doubt on the development of this market. For example, Aon expressed disappointment that more of a CNBR market had not developed with TRIA in place.[236] This demonstrates that even with the offer of Federal participation in CNBR risk, insurers do not wish to cover such risks. As AIG stated: "In general, the insurance industry has not historically provided coverage for loss to commercial property arising from a nuclear event and it is highly unlikely that it will provide such coverage in the future."[237] Aon put it this way: "Basically, the (re)insurance industry views CNBR event exposure as a 'company killer' where the potential gross aggregate PML (probable maximum loss) is well in excess of the industry's entire capital base."[238]

Conclusion

The factors determining the availability and affordability of CNBR coverage in the marketplace have more to do with the nature, scale, and uncertainty of the damage and losses from CNBR events – however caused – and less to do with terrorism specifically. Most of the coverage that exists today is tied to state mandates, most prominently workers' compensation insurance and some aspects of fire insurance through the Standard Fire Policy. Even with TRIA in place – which covers CNBR terrorist losses but does not mandate that insurers provide it – insurers by and large continue to avoid this risk as has historically been the case. There is virtually no CNBR reinsurance available, and the modeling issues both for exposure and probability become even more complicated for CNBR. Given the general reluctance of insurance companies to provide coverage for these types of risks, there may be little potential for future market development.

D.2. Buyer Behavior

Policyholder Perception of CNBR Risks

The 2005 Treasury study found that only 35 percent of insurers offered some form of CNBR coverage in some of their policies (not including workers' compensation).[239] Even with the availability of a Federal backstop, insurers generally continued to exclude CNBR where state law permitted it. Moreover, there has been very little take-up of what has been available. A recent survey of corporate risk managers revealed that roughly 90 percent reported having no coverage for CNBR attacks, with less than 10 percent having coverage.[240]

---

[236] Aon Corporation, Comments to the PWG dated April 21, 2006.

[237] American International Group, Inc., Comments to the PWG dated April 21, 2006.

[238] Aon Corporation, Comments to the PWG dated April 21, 2006.

[239] U.S. Department of Treasury, Report to Congress, "Assessment: The Terrorism Risk Insurance Act of 2002," (June 30, 2005), p. 77.

[240] Risk and Insurance Management Society, Inc., Member Survey: Terrorism Coverage (July 13, 2006).

The 2005 Treasury study revealed that less than 3 percent of policyholders purchased CNBR terrorism risk coverage (not including workers' compensation) in 2002, 2003, and 2004. Of the policyholders that did not purchase CNBR coverage, 85 percent in 2003 and 64 percent in 2004 indicated that not being at risk was a reason for not purchasing CNBR coverage. In contrast, 61 percent in 2003 and 26 percent in 2004 indicated that high premiums was a reason for not purchasing CNBR coverage. Other factors, such as restrictive terms and inadequate coverage, were not widely found to be reasons for not purchasing CNBR coverage.[241] Take-up could also be affected by expectations that the Federal government would provide Federal disaster assistance following a catastrophic CNBR event.[242]

Conclusion

Some insurance consumers have expressed an interest in purchasing CNBR coverage, but with the limited capacity and relatively high prices, many have decided to forgo such purchases. Policyholder expectations regarding lack of potential exposure and likelihood of post-disaster Federal aid are probably higher for CNBR risks than for relatively smaller-scale conventional terrorist attacks. The 2005 Treasury study found that the main reasons for not purchasing CNBR terrorism coverage was that policyholders believed either that they were not at risk or that the premiums were too high. Unless these expectations change and policyholders are willing to pay higher prices, the potential for further development of coverage for CNBR terrorism coverage will be limited.

III. Overall Conclusion

The market for terrorism risk insurance in the U.S. fundamentally changed following September 11. Insurance coverage that was generally provided for free prior to September 11, became subject to capacity limits and pricing became relatively expensive. The Federal government responded by enacting and extending a government reinsurance program in the form of TRIA.

While there are inherent difficulties in evaluating the long-term nature of the terrorism risk insurance market with a government program in place, a number of positive developments have occurred in the overall terrorism risk insurance market since September 11: improvements in the ability of insurers to model terrorism risk exposure;

---

[241] U.S. Department of Treasury, Report to Congress, "Assessment: The Terrorism Risk Insurance Act of 2002," (June 30, 2005), pp. 105-106.

[242] Wharton Risk Management and Decision Processes Center, "TRIA and Beyond," The Wharton School, University of Pennsylvania, August 2005; Dixon, et al., Occasional Paper, "Issues and Options for Government Intervention in the Market for Terrorism Insurance," RAND Center for Terrorism Risk Management Policy, 2004, p. 10; Howard Kunreuther & Erwann Michel-Kerjan, "Dealing with Extreme Events: New Challenges for Terrorism Risk Coverage in the U.S.," Wharton Risk Management and Decision Processes Center, April 2004, p. 20; Robert Rhee, "Terrorism Risk in a Post-9/11 Economy: The Convergence of Capital Markets, Insurance, and Government Action," *Arizona State Law Journal*, Vol. 37, No. 2 (2005).

an increase in reinsurance capacity; improved financial health of the insurance industry and a willingness to underwrite additional terrorism risk insurance; generally falling or stable prices for terrorism risk insurance even as insurers' retention of risk has increased; and increased buyer demand for coverage. Further improvements in insurers' ability to model and manage terrorism risk and the other factors noted above, will likely contribute to the long-term development of the terrorism risk insurance market. However, the greater uncertainty associated with predicting the frequency of terrorist attacks along with what appears to be a general unwillingness of some insurance policyholders to purchase terrorism risk insurance coverage makes any evaluation of the potential degree of long-term development of the terrorism risk insurance market somewhat difficult.

In contrast to the overall market for terrorism risk insurance, there has been little development in the terrorism risk insurance market for CNBR risks since September 11. Given that insurance companies have historically excluded coverage for these types of losses – even if not caused by terrorism – there may be little potential for future market development.

Finally, there has been little to no disruption in the group life insurance market since September 11, even though group life insurers do not have access to the TRIA Program. While group life insurers face some of the same issues as property and casualty insurers in terms of managing aggregation exposures and reinsurance availability, based on what appears to be a highly competitive market today there is no reason to expect that those market conditions will not continue in the long term.

* * *

Appendix

Maritime Administration, MAR–830, Room 7201, 400 Seventh St., SW., Washington, DC 20590; *richard.lolich@dot.gov.*

(Authority: 5 U.S.C. App 2, Sec. 9(a)(2); 41 CFR 101–6. 1005; DOT Order 1120.3B)

Dated: March 1, 2006.

Joel C. Richard,
Secretary, Maritime Administration.

[FR Doc. E6–3151 Filed 3–6–06; 8:45 am]

BILLING CODE 4910–81–P

DEPARTMENT OF THE TREASURY

Analysis by the President's Working Group on Financial Markets on the Long-Term Availability and Affordability of Insurance for Terrorism Risk

AGENCY: Department of the Treasury, Departmental Offices.

ACTION: Notice; request for comments.

SUMMARY: The Terrorism Risk Insurance Extension Act of 2005 requires the President's Working Group on Financial Markets to perform an analysis regarding the long-term availability and affordability of insurance for terrorism risk, including group life coverage and coverage for chemical, nuclear, biological, and radiological events.

As chair of the President's Working Group, Treasury is issuing this notice seeking public comment to assist the President's Working Group in its analysis.

DATES: Comments must be in writing and received by April 21, 2006.

ADDRESSES: Please submit comments (if hard copy, preferably an original and two copies) to Treasury's Office of Financial Institutions Policy, Attention: President's Working Group on Financial Markets Public Comment Record, Room 3160 Annex, Department of the Treasury, 1500 Pennsylvania Avenue, NW., Washington, DC 20220. Because postal mail may be subject to processing delay, we recommend that comments be submitted by electronic mail to: *PWGComments@do.treas.gov.* All comments should be captioned with "President's Working Group on Financial Markets: Terrorism Risk Insurance Analysis." Please include your name, affiliation, address, e-mail address and telephone number(s) in your comment. Where appropriate, comments should include a short Executive Summary (no more than five single-spaced pages). All comments received will be available for public inspection by appointment only at the Reading Room of the Treasury Library.

To make appointments, please call one of the numbers below.

FOR FURTHER INFORMATION CONTACT: C. Christopher Ledoux, Senior Policy Analyst, Office of Financial Institutions Policy, 202–622–6813; or Mario Ugoletti, Director, Office of Financial Institutions Policy, 202–622–2730 (not toll free numbers).

SUPPLEMENTARY INFORMATION: On November 26, 2002, the President signed into law the Terrorism Risk Insurance Act of 2002 (Pub. L. 107–297, 116 Stat. 2322) (hereinafter referenced as "TRIA"). TRIA's purposes are to address market disruptions, ensure the continued widespread availability and affordability of commercial property and casualty insurance for terrorism risk, and to allow for a transition period for the private markets to stabilize and build capacity while preserving state insurance regulation and consumer protections. Title I of TRIA established a temporary Federal program of shared public and private compensation for insured commercial property and casualty losses resulting from an act of terrorism, as defined in the Act. TRIA authorized Treasury to administer and implement the Terrorism Risk Insurance Program (Program), including the issuance of regulations and procedures. As originally enacted, the Program was to end on December 31, 2005.

Congress subsequently approved and on December 22, 2005, the President signed into law the Terrorism Risk Insurance Extension Act of 2005 (Pub. L. 109–144, 119 Stat. 2660) (the Extension Act). The Extension Act continued the Program for two years until December 31, 2007, revised several structural aspects of the Program, and required an analysis of the availability and affordability of terrorism risk insurance. Specifically, the Extension Act amended section 108 of TRIA to require the President's Working Group on Financial Markets,[1] in consultation with the National Association of Insurance Commissioners, representatives of the insurance industry, representatives of the securities industry, and representatives of policy holders, to perform an analysis regarding the long-term availability and affordability of insurance for terrorism risk, including group life coverage and coverage for chemical, nuclear, biological, and radiological events. This Notice seeks comment from these and

[1] The President's Working Group on Financial Markets (established by Executive Order 12631) is comprised of the Secretary of the Treasury (who serves as its Chairman), the Chairman of the Federal Reserve Board, the Chairman of the Securities and Exchange Commission, and the Chairman of the Commodity Futures Trading Commission.

any other interested parties as a means of satisfying the consultation requirement in the most open and efficient manner. TRIA, as amended by the Extension Act, requires the President's Working Group on Financial Markets to submit a report to Congress on its findings no later than September 30, 2006.

Treasury, on behalf of the President's Working Group, is soliciting comments, including empirical data and other information in support of such comments, where appropriate and available, regarding the long-term availability and affordability of insurance for terrorism risk, including terrorism risk insurance coverage for group life and for chemical, nuclear, biological, and radiological events. We request that submitters distinguish between risk from foreign and domestic terrorism in their comments. In addition, we seek and solicit comment in response to the following specific questions:

I. Long-Term Availability and Affordability of Terrorism Risk Insurance

1.1 In the long-term, what are the key factors that will determine the availability and affordability of terrorism risk insurance coverage? How can these factors be measured and projected?

1.2 What improvements have taken place in the ability of insurers to measure and manage their accumulation of terrorism risk exposures? How will this evolve in the long-term?

1.3 What improvements have taken place in the ability of insurers to price terrorism risk insurance, including in the development and use of modeling? How will this evolve in the long-term?

1.4 How, if at all, were primary insurers' pricing decisions affected by the anticipated expiration of TRIA at the end of 2005, particularly for insurance policies extending into 2006 that cover terrorism risk? What role did the pricing and availability of reinsurance play in those decisions?

1.5 What role do mitigation efforts related to terrorism risk play in an insurer's underwriting and pricing decisions? How will this evolve in the long-term?

1.6 What is the current availability of reinsurance to cover terrorism risk? Please distinguish by line or type of insurance being reinsured and on what basis (treaty or facultative). How will this evolve in the long-term?

1.7 At what policyholder retention levels are insurance programs being structured to cover terrorism risk; and, with regard to insurers, how are reinsurance programs likewise being structured? Please comment on the availability and affordability at each level.

1.8   In the long-term, what are the key factors that will determine the amount of private-market insurer and reinsurer capacity available for terrorism risk insurance coverage? How will this evolve in the long-term? Please comment on potential entry of new capital into insurance markets.

1.9   To what extent have alternate risk transfer methods (e.g., catastrophe bonds or other capital market instruments) been used for terrorism risk insurance, and what is the potential for the long-term development of these products?

1.10   To what extent have captive insurance companies been used for terrorism risk insurance, and what is the potential for the use of captive insurers to insure against such risk long-term?

1.11   Have state approaches made coverage more or less available and affordable, such as through permitted exclusions and rate regulation? To what extent will the long-term availability and affordability of terrorism risk insurance be influenced by state insurance regulation? Please comment on state approaches to ensure the continued availability and affordability of terrorism risk insurance in the absence of the TRIA Program being in-place (include state approaches after September 11, 2001 and before TRIA became law on November 24, 2002, as well as state approaches in preparation for the expiration of the TRIA Program).

1.12   What are the differences in availability and affordability of terrorism risk insurance between the licensed/admitted market and the non-admitted/surplus lines market, and, if so, to what degree are those changes attributable to the degree and manner in which each market is regulated?

1.13   What are the differences in availability and affordability of terrorism risk insurance coverage for losses at U.S. locations as compared to such coverage for losses at non-US locations?

II. Long-Term Availability and Affordability of Group Life Insurance Coverage

2.1   What impact, if any, does terrorism risk have on the availability and affordability of group life insurance coverage to the policy holder (e.g., employer) and certificate holders (e.g., employees)? How will this evolve in the long-term?

2.2   To what extent is an insurer's decision to issue group life coverage influenced by aggregation or

accumulation risk in certain locations? What steps have group life insurance providers taken or do they plan to take to offset any aggregation or accumulation risk?

2.3   Has terrorism risk made group life coverage less affordable to the policy or certificate holder? Have group life insurance rates increased or decreased as compared to rates before and since September 11, 2001?

2.4   Please explain how group life insurance coverage may be bundled with other coverages and benefits provided through an employee-benefits program, and how group life coverage is priced, either separately or collectively, through such programs. Please describe any effects competition has on such pricing.

2.5   Are group life providers voluntarily providing coverage for loss of life arising out of or resulting from acts of terrorism, or is coverage mandated by any state or federal laws? Are group life providers prohibited by law from excluding terrorism risk from group life insurance policies?

2.6   Has terrorism risk affected segments of the group life market differently, such as in the case of small/ medium sized employers, and if so, why?

2.7   In the long-term, what are the key factors that will determine the availability and affordability of terrorism risk insurance coverage for group life insurance?

III. Long-Term Availability and Affordability of Insurance Coverage for Chemical, Nuclear, Biological, and Radiological (CNBR) [2] Events Caused by Terrorism

3.1   What is the current availability and affordability of coverage for CNBR events, and for what perils is coverage available, subject to what limits, and under what policy terms and conditions? Is there a difference in the availability and affordability of coverage for CNBR events caused by acts of terrorism?

3.2   What was the general availability of coverage for CNBR events prior to the terrorist attack of September 11, 2001? To what extent, subject to what limits, and for what perils was coverage available? Did it cover acts of terrorism?

3.3   If coverage for CNBR events caused by acts of terrorism is available, please describe generally to what extent (i.e., limits, locations, exclusions, etc.)

for what kinds of insurance and from what types of insurers (i.e., large/small, admitted/surplus lines, etc.). How will this evolve in the long-term?

3.4   To what extent is terrorism risk coverage available and affordable for nuclear facilities and for chemical plants, manufacturers, and industrial chemical users?

3.5   To what extent, both prior to and since September 11, 2001, have various states allowed insurers to exclude coverage for CNBR events? Please comment on requirements for workers' compensation and fire-following coverage.

3.6   It appears that some insurers are unwilling to provide coverage for CNBR events caused by acts of terrorism even with the federal loss sharing provided by the TRIA Program. Why would this be the case given that TRIA limits an insurer's maximum loss exposure?

3.7   In the long-term, what are the key factors that will determine the availability and affordability of terrorism risk insurance coverage for CNBR events?

Dated: February 27, 2006.

Emil W. Henry, Jr.,
Assistant Secretary of the Treasury.
[FR Doc. E6–3150 Filed 3–6–06; 8:45 am]
BILLING CODE 4811–37–P

DEPARTMENT OF VETERANS AFFAIRS

Veterans' Disability Benefits Commission; Amendment Notice of Meeting (FR Doc. 06–1514 Filed 2–16–06; 8:45 a.m.)

The Department of Veterans Affairs (VA) gives notice under Public Law 92–463 (Federal Advisory Committee Act) that the Veterans' Disability Benefits Commission meeting scheduled on March 16–17, 2006, at the Holiday Inn National Airport, 2650 Jefferson Davis Highway, Arlington, VA, will begin each day at 8 a.m. instead of 8:30 a.m. to allow more time for Commission discussion.

For additional information, please contact Mr. Ray Wilburn, Executive Director, Veterans' Disability Benefits Commission, 1101 Pennsylvania Avenue, NW., 5th Floor, Washington, DC 20004, or by e-mail at *veterans@vets commission.intranets.com.*

Dated: February 27, 2006.

By Direction of the Secretary.

E. Philip Riggin,
Committee Management Officer.
[FR Doc. 06–2109 Filed 3–6–06; 8:45 am]
BILLING CODE 8320–01–M

---

[2] Though CNBR is commonly used to refer collectively to chemical, nuclear, biological, and radiological losses, comments can be narrow in addressing any of the coverages. If the comment makes such a distinction, please make clear which coverage is being addressed.

PROPERTY AND CASUALTY COMMERCIAL LINES RE-ENGINEERING

The date following each state indicates the last time information for the state was reviewed/changed.

STATE	CITATION	CRITERIA FOR EXEMPTION	EXEMPTION FROM WHAT REQUIREMENTS
AL	No provision		
AK	§ 21.39.040	The statute gives authority for the director to adopt regulations consistent with the NAIC Property and Casualty Rate and Policy Form Model Act.	
AZ	No provision		
AR	§§ 23-67-206, 23-79-109	Property and casualty insurance for large commercial risks, excluding workers' compensation, employers liability and professional liability. Large commercial risk means an insured with: • Total premium of $250,000 or more for property and casualty insurance; and • At least 25 employees; and • Full time risk manager.	Rate and form filing.
CA	No provision		
CO	§§ 10-4-1401 to 10-4-1404 Ins. Reg. 5-1-13	Commissioner shall adopt regulation defining what organizations and entities qualify as exempt commercial policyholders. Commissioner shall mandate that exempt commercial policyholders procure insurance through a risk manager. Exempt commercial policyholder means a person that procures fire, casualty, inland marine, etc. insurance through the use of a risk manager. Does not include title insurance or worker's compensation coverage. Must meet at least one of the following: • Aggregate premiums of $50,000 during most recent year • Net worth of $10 million • Net sales or renewal of $10 million • At least 25 full-time employees • If a nonprofit, annual operating budget of at least $2.5 million; or, if a public entity, annual operating budget of $10 million • If a municipality, has a population of at least 20,000	Rate filing and approval, form certification requirements.

PROPERTY AND CASUALTY COMMERCIAL LINES RE-ENGINEERING

STATE	CITATION	CRITERIA FOR EXEMPTION	EXEMPTION FROM WHAT REQUIREMENTS
CT	No provision		
DE	No provision		
DC (2/04)	§§ 31-2701, 31-2714	An "exempt commercial risk" is an entity that meets one of the following criteria: • Retains a risk manager; • Net worth over $2 million; • Annual revenues in excess of $2 million; • 10 or more employees; • Aggregate insurance premiums over $10,000; • Insured property value of $2 million or more; or • Is a not-for-profit or public body generating annual budgeted expenditures of at least $5 million.	Rate and form filing.
FL	No provision		
GA.	Reg. ch. 120-2-77	Large commercial risks meet all these criteria: • 25 or more full-time employee; • $1.5 million or more in assets; • annual revenue of $2.5 million or more; and • Annual P/C premiums from Georgia operations in excess of $50,000 or $250,000 for risks with multistate locations	Rate filing.

PROPERTY AND CASUALTY COMMERCIAL LINES RE-ENGINEERING

STATE	CITATION	CRITERIA FOR EXEMPTION	EXEMPTION FROM WHAT REQUIREMENTS
HI	No provision		
ID	No provision		
IL	Illinois is a no-file state.		
IN (8/03)	§§ 27-1-22-2.5 to 27-1-22-4	Exempt commercial policyholder meets three of these criteria: • Not worth over $25 million; • Net revenue or sales over $50 million; • More than 25 employees for a company or 50 or more for holding company; • Aggregate yearly commercial premium of more than $75,000 (excluding workers' compensation and professional liability); • Nonprofit or public entity with annual budget of at least $25 million; and • Buys insurance through a risk manager.	Rate and form filing.
IA	No provision		
KS	§ 40-955	Except for workers' compensation and employer's liability lines, the following commercial line risks are exempt from filing: • Risks written on an excess or umbrella basis; • Commercial risks not rated according to manual, rating plans or schedule; • Large risks; • Special risks designated by the commissioner. Large risk means the insured has: • Total insured property value of $5 million or more; • Total annual gross revenues of $10 million or more; and • In preceding year a total paid premium of $50,000 or more for property insurance, $50,000 or more for general liability insurance, or $100,000 or more for multiple lines policies.	Rate filing.

PROPERTY AND CASUALTY COMMERCIAL LINES RE-ENGINEERING

STATE	CITATION	CRITERIA FOR EXEMPTION	EXEMPTION FROM WHAT REQUIREMENTS

KY	§ 304.11-020	Exempts policies sold to industrial insureds, government entity insureds and exempt commercial policyholders.
		
		"Industrial insured" is an insured that:
		• Uses full-time employee acting as insurance manager or buyer
		• $25,000 or more annual premiums
		• At least 25 full-time employees
		• Already considered industrial insured.
		"Government entity insured" is an insured that:
		• Is located in city or county with population of at least 50,000
		• Uses full-time employee acting as insurance manager or buyer
		• At least $100,000 in premiums, excluding life, health, annuity
		• At least 50 full-time employees
		• Satisfies criteria in regulation
		"Exempt commercial policyholder" means an insured that:
		• Uses full-time employee as an insurance manager or buyer; and
		• City or county with population over 50,000 or a not-for-profit with yearly budget over $25 million, or
		• Meets all four of the following criteria:
		  • $500,000 premiums
		  • Net worth of $25 million
		  • Net revenue or sales of $50 million in prior year
		  • 100 employees or 200 for holding company
			Rate and form filing.

PROPERTY AND CASUALTY COMMERCIAL LINES RE-ENGINEERING

STATE	CITATION	CRITERIA FOR EXEMPTION	EXEMPTION FROM WHAT REQUIREMENTS
LA (5/05)	§ 22:620; Reg. 37:XIII.9001 to 37:XIII.9021 (Reg. 72)	Special commercial entities, as defined by the commissioner by regulation. An exempt commercial policyholder meets the following criteria: • Aggregate premium, excluding workers' compensation and employers' liability of more than $200,000 a year, • Not less than 50 employees, or 100 for affiliated group; • If a municipality, not less than 50,000 population; • If a public entity, an operating budget of not less than $20 million; • Must sign certification form acknowledging form filing is exempt from review by the dept.	Form filing.
	§ 22:1401.1; Reg. 37:XIII.9301 to 37:XIII.9319 (Reg. 80)	If have at least $10,000 in annual premiums, file rates for informational purposes only in a competitive marketplace. Does not apply to workers' compensation or medical malpractice.	Rate filing.
ME (5/05)	tit. 24-A § 2412-A	• Policyholder must utilize a risk manager to procure insurance • Must have aggregate premiums of $50,000 or more, excluding worker's compensation, medical malpractice, life, health and disability In addition must meet two of these three criteria: • Net worth of $10 million • Net revenue of $5 million • More than 25 employees or over 50 for holding company	Rate and form filing approval requirements.
MD	Ins. § 11-206	"Exempt commercial policyholder" is one paying at least $75,000 in annual premiums and meeting two of the following criteria: • Annual revenue of $10 million • Net worth of $5 million • At least 25 full-time employees • Nonprofit with annual budget of at least $10 million • Municipality of at least 15,000 population	Policy forms, except workers' compensation.

PROPERTY AND CASUALTY COMMERCIAL LINES RE-ENGINEERING

STATE	CITATION	CRITERIA FOR EXEMPTION	EXEMPTION FROM WHAT REQUIREMENTS
MA (8/04)	§§ 175.224 to 175.225	Large commercial policyholder must have aggregate $30,000 premiums excluding workers' compensation and meet at least 2 of the following: • Net worth of $10 million • Net revenue or sales of $5 million • At least 25 employees per company or 50 per holding company aggregate • Nonprofit or public entity with budget or assets of $25 million • Municipality of 20,000 or more population • Retains a full-time risk manager with certain credentials	Rate and form filing
MI	No provision		
MN	No provision		
MS	No provision		
MO (2/03)	§§ 379.321	Commercial casualty insurance is defined as that procured for a business or nonprofit organization. Commercial property is defined as property insurance for business and professional interests.	File rates for informational purposes only.
MT	No provision		

PROPERTY AND CASUALTY COMMERCIAL LINES RE-ENGINEERING

STATE	CITATION	CRITERIA FOR EXEMPTION	EXEMPTION FROM WHAT REQUIREMENTS
NE	Reg. tit. 210 ch. 73	The regulation sets up 3 classes of exempt commercial policyholders: (1) either: – Uses a risk manager, – Generates at least $100,000 in aggregate commercial lines P/C premiums yearly and – Meets at least two of the following conditions: – $250,000 in premiums, excluding worker's compensation and medical professional liability or $1 million in premium including the above, – net worth of at least $25 million, – net revenue or sales at least $50 million, – employs at least 250, – if a not-for-profit or government entity, budget of at least $25 million. or – generates at least $100,000 in aggregate premiums, and – in a jurisdiction with greater aggregate premiums than Nebraska, – not required to use rating manuals – not required to use filed forms – access to surplus lines not limited to a requirement that not available from licensed insurer. (2) must meet one of these sets of conditions: – Uses a risk manager and generates $50,000 in premiums; – $250,000 in premiums, excluding worker's compensation and medical professional liability or $1 million in premium including the above, – $50,000 in premiums and, in a jurisdiction with greater premiums than Nebraska, not subject to rating manuals or form filing requirements. (3) must meet one of these sets of conditions: – Uses a risk manager and generates $25,000 in premiums; – $100,000 in premiums, excluding worker's compensation and medical professional liability or $250,000 in premium including the above – $25,000 in premiums and, in a jurisdiction with greater premiums than Nebraska, not subject to rating manuals.	Exempt from rate and form filing except for workers' compensation and auto liability. Surplus lines doesn't require demonstration that coverage not available. Exempt from rate and form filing. Exempt from rate filing requirements.

PROPERTY AND CASUALTY COMMERCIAL LINES RE-ENGINEERING

STATE	CITATION	CRITERIA FOR EXEMPTION	EXEMPTION FROM WHAT REQUIREMENTS
NV	No provision		

NH	§ 414:4	Filing requirements do not apply to policies issued to large scale commercial insured. Defined as insured that:
		• Pays annual aggregate insurance premiums of $500,000 or more; and
		• Meets any of the following additional criteria:
		  – Net revenues or sales annually in excess of $100 million;
		  – Employs more than 500 employees per individual insured or 1000 employees in the aggregate;
		  – Full-time employee acts as insurance manager or retain qualified insurance consultant;
		  – Net worth in excess of $50 million;
		  – Not-for-profit or public agency with annual budget of at least $45 million; and
		  – Municipality with population of more than 50,000.
			Rate filing.

NJ	No provision		
NM (2/05)	§ 59A-18-12 Reg. 13.8.2.26	Authority to exempt some market segments from rate regulation law. Filings exempt from prior approval if for commercial insurance (except workers compensation, medical liability, or ski basin liability) and the filing does not result in a renewal rate change greater than 25% for a policyholder with current premiums less than $10,000.	
NY	No provision		
NC	No provision		
ND	No provision		

PROPERTY AND CASUALTY COMMERCIAL LINES RE-ENGINEERING

STATE	CITATION	CRITERIA FOR EXEMPTION	EXEMPTION FROM WHAT REQUIREMENTS
OH	No provision		
OK	tit. 36 § 997	Following categories of commercial lines risks are special risks and are exempt: • Risks written on excess or umbrella basis • Commercial lines insurance risks not rated according to manual, rating plan or schedules • Commercial lines insurance risks with minimum annual premium total of $10,000 • Specifically designated special risks (commercial aviation, credit, boiler, inland marine, surety, etc.)	Rate filing.
OR	No provision		
PA	§§ 40-66-101 to 40-66-119	Large commercial risk is one whose aggregate premium, excluding workers' compensation, totals at least $25,000, or that has at least 25 employees, and for which the entity uses a risk manager. Commissioner may adjust these numbers by regulation. Commissioner may require filing for large commercial risks in noncompetitive market.	Rate and form filings.
RI	§§ 27-65-1 to 27-65-2	Commercial policyholders exempt if use a risk manager and meet any two of these criteria: • Net worth over $50 million • Net revenue or sales over $100 million • More than 500 employees per company or 1,000 employees per holding company aggregate • Aggregate premium over $150,000, excluding workers' compensation, health and professional liability	Rate and form filing requirements.
SC (2/04)	§§ 38-1-20; 38-61-25; Ins. Reg. 69-64	Exempts rates filing for commercial policyholders as set by commissioner. Commissioner may set other standards by regulation.	Rate filing.

PROPERTY AND CASUALTY COMMERCIAL LINES RE-ENGINEERING

STATE	CITATION	CRITERIA FOR EXEMPTION	EXEMPTION FROM WHAT REQUIREMENTS
SD (8/05)	§§ 58-24-68 to 58-24-74	Exempt commercial policyholder is one that uses a risk manager and meets at least 2 of the following: • Has purchased at least $100,000 of insurance in past year; • Net worth of at least $10 million • Net sales or revenue of at least $10 million on last financial statement; • At least 100 full-time employees; • If a nonprofit, an annual budget of at least $2.5 million; • If a public entity, an operating budget of at least $10 million; • If a municipality, a population of at least 20,000.	Rate and form filing.
TN	No provision		
TX	No provision		
UT	No provision		
VT	No provision		
VA (8/05)	§ 38.2-1903.1	Exempts large commercial policyholder that uses a risk manager. Must meet two of the following six criteria: • Net worth over $2 million • Annual revenue over $2 million • More than 10 employees • Nonprofit with budget of $5 million • Municipality with population exceeding 30,000 • Pays aggregate insurance premiums in excess of $25,000	Rate and form filing for worker's compensation and professional liability issued to large commercial risks; form filings for commercial auto policies issued to large commercial risks.

PROPERTY AND CASUALTY COMMERCIAL LINES RE-ENGINEERING

STATE	CITATION	CRITERIA FOR EXEMPTION	EXEMPTION FROM WHAT REQUIREMENTS
WA (2/04)	Reg. 284-24-120	Rate filing requirements are suspended with respect to large commercial property/casualty accounts. Defined as an account with enough insurance-buying experience to negotiate in a largely unregulated environment. Must meet two of the following criteria: • Annual premium of $100,000 or more excluding workers' compensation • Net revenues in excess of $100 million • More than 200 employers • Net worth over $50 million • Not-for-profit with budget or assets of at least $45 million • Municipality with a population over 50,000	Rates
WV (8/05)	§ 33-6-8	Commercial lines property and casualty form filings are file and use; does not include medical malpractice.	Forms
	§ 33-20-4	Commercial lines property and casualty rate filings are file and use; does not include medical malpractice.	Rates
WI	No provision		
WY	No provision		

This chart does not constitute a formal legal opinion by the NAIC staff on the provisions of state law and should not be relied upon as such. Every effort has been made to provide correct and accurate summaries to assist the reader in targeting useful information. For further details, the statutes and regulations cited should be consulted. The NAIC attempts to provide current information; however, readers should consult state law for additional adoptions.

Standard Fire Policy States

STATE	USES SFP?	TERRORISM EXCLUSION?	ENACTED SINCE 9/11
Alabama	No		
Alaska	No		
Arizona	Yes	Commercial Lines Only	2005
Arkansas	No		
California	Yes	No	
Colorado	No		
Connecticut	Yes	Commercial Lines Only Only while TRIA in effect	2004
Delaware	No		
DC	No		
Florida	No		
Georgia	Yes	No	
Hawaii	Yes	No	
Idaho	Yes	Commercial Lines Only Foreign Terrorism Only	2005
Illinois	Yes	No	
Indiana	No		
Iowa	Yes	No	
Kansas	No		
Kentucky	No		
Louisiana	Yes	Commercial Lines Only	2003
Maine	Yes	No	
Maryland	No		
Massachusetts	Yes	No	
Michigan	Yes	Commercial Lines Only	2003
Minnesota	Yes	Commercial Lines Only	2003
Mississippi	No		
Missouri	Yes	No	
Montana	No		
Nebraska	Yes	Commercial Lines Only	2003
Nevada	No		
New Hampshire	Yes	Fire or Other Perils	2003
New Jersey	Yes	No	
New Mexico	No		
New York	Yes	No	
North Carolina	Yes	No	
North Dakota	Yes	Commercial Lines Only	2005
Ohio	No		
Oklahoma	Yes	Commissioner Discretion	2003
Oregon	Yes	No	
Pennsylvania	Yes	No	
Rhode Island	Yes	Commercial Lines Only	2004
South Carolina	No		
South Dakota	No		
Tennessee	No		
Texas	No		
Utah	No		
Vermont	No		
Virginia	Yes	Commercial Lines Only Only while TRIA in effect	2003
Washington	Yes	No	
West Virginia	Yes	No	
Wisconsin	Yes	No	
Wyoming	No		

Source: NAIC